W9-CHR-167

This Tree Grows Out of Hell

This Tree Grows Out of Hell

Mesoamerica and the Search for the Magical Body

Ptolemy Tompkins

HarperSanFrancisco

A Division of HarperCollins*Publishers*

Frontispiece: *Detail of the ruins at Palenque by Catherwood, from Stephens'* Incidents of Travel in Central America, Chiapas and Yucatan.

Grateful acknowledgment is made for permission to reprint excerpts from the following works:
Cantares Mexicanos: Songs of the Aztecs, translated from the Nahuatl, with an Introduction and Commentary by John Bierhorst, with the permission of the publishers, Stanford University Press. Copyright © 1985 by the Trustees of the Leland Stanford Junior University.

From *The Kabir Book* by Robert Bly. Copyright © 1971, 1977 by Robert Bly and the Seventies Press. Reprinted by permission of Beacon Press.

Credits continue on page 190

THIS TREE GROWS OUT OF HELL: *Mesoamerica and the Search for the Magical Body.* Copyright © 1990 by Ptolemy Tompkins. All rights reserved. Printed in the United States of America. No part of this book may be used or reproduced in any manner whatsoever without written permission except in the case of brief quotations embodied in critical articles and reviews. For information address HarperCollins Publishers, 10 East 53rd Street, New York, NY 10022.

FIRST EDITION

Library of Congress Cataloging-in-Publication Data

Tompkins, Ptolemy.
   This tree grows out of hell : Mesoamerica and the search for the magical body / Ptolemy Tompkins.—1st ed.
      p.   cm.
   Includes bibliographical references.
   ISBN 0-06-250866-0 (alk. paper) :
   1. Aztecs—Religion and mythology.   2. Mayas—Religion and mythology.   3. Indians of Mexico—Religion and mythology.
4. Indians of Central America—Religion and mythology.   I. Title.
F1219.76.R45T47   1990
299'.792—dc20   89-46461
                                                                                     CIP

90   91   92   93   94   HAD   10   9   8   7   6   5   4   3   2   1

This edition is printed on acid-free paper that meets the American National Standards Institute Z39.48 Standard.

For Maria Teresa

Contents

A Note on the Title

SEVERAL READERS OF THIS BOOK in manuscript have expressed puzzlement at the title. What exactly do I mean when I say *this* tree, and what sort of hell am I claiming it to grow out of? Though the word predates Christianity, for most people "Hell" conjures up a specifically Christian place, and I perhaps would have been wiser to use a Native American term for the underworld such as the Mayan "Xibalba" or the Aztec "Mictlan." Neither of these roll off the tongue with the ease that "Hell" does, however, so for the sake of esthetics I decided to stay with this term despite its heavy Christian connotations.

The tree of the title is a general reference to the world tree, or *axis mundi*, which, throughout Mesoamerica and the ancient world in general, served as one of the most popular ciphers for designating the universe. The lore of the world tree is extensive, and there are any number of possible explanations for this analogy. For my purposes, however, one stood out in particular: trees are living organisms comprised of three separate yet intimately connected parts. Even without a sophisticated knowledge of the complex chemical interplay carried on via the capillaries of the trunk between the roots buried in the ground and the branches and leaves that spread out far above them, it must have been clear to the early human observer that each of a tree's three general areas somehow needed the others in order for the whole to continue to flourish. Likewise, the tripartite world of over-, middle-, and underworld, which together comprised the universe of the ancient Mesoamerican and which the image of the tree so admirably stood for, demanded a similar situation of continuous fruitful interaction.

As I try to show in the following pages, many of the disasters that beset Mesoamerican civilization throughout the centuries of its growth can be understood as resulting from breakdowns in this system of constant circulation and interpenetration. Like the invisible matrix of roots that feed nutrients to a tree's trunk and branches in exchange for the fruits of photosynthesis, the labyrinthian underworlds of the Mesoamerican cosmos held powerful spiritual forces without which the middle world of mortals and the upper, "angelic" realms to which the souls of those mortals ultimately aspired could not long function properly. Modern psychological theory is thinking in similar terms when it suggests that the psyche is itself comprised of three or more generalized areas or levels. The "lower" regions of the psyche are described in many models as being dark and initially unappealing, yet it is generally agreed that these regions must nevertheless be courted and addressed openly if real psychic growth is to take place. It was out of an appreciation for this ancient and variously stated belief that, both in the microcosm of the human psyche and the macrocosm of the universe itself, what grows toward light does so through and by means of darkness that I arrived at the formulation of my title—this tree grows out of hell.

Ptolemy Tompkins

List of Illustrations

1. Detail of the ruins at Palenque by Catherwood, from Stephens' *Incidents of Travel in Central America, Chiapas and Yucatan.* (Frontispiece.)

2. Detail by Catherwood of ruins at the Maya city of Tulum on the Yucatan coast.

3. A Maya battle scene from the eighth century A.D. The smaller figures at center are rival warriors being taken captive. (Yaxchilán Lintel 8 from *Corpus of Maya Hieroglyphic Inscriptions, Vol. 3, Part 1*, by Ian Graham and Eric von Euw. Copyright © 1977 by Peabody Museum of Archaeology and Ethnology, Harvard University. Cambridge, Massachusetts.)

4. Pacal's tomb-lid featuring the world tree with celestial bird at the top and the gaping, stylized jaws of the underworld at bottom. (Copyright © 1980 by Merle Greene Robertson. Used courtesy of Merle Greene Robertson.)

5. Lady Xoc, with the subterranean vision serpent rising before her. (Yaxchilán Lintel 25 from *Corpus of Maya Hieroglyphic Inscriptions, Vol. 3, Part 1*, by Ian Graham and Eric von Euw. Copyright © 1977 by Peabody Museum of Archaeology and Ethnology, Harvard University. Cambridge, Massachusetts.)

6. Hunahpu prepares to decapitate his brother Xbalanque in the depths of Xibalba. Illustration from a Classic Maya vase currently on display at the Metropolitan Museum of Art. (Courtesy of Michael Coe and the Grollier Club.)

7. Four characteristically death-oriented images from the *Codex Laud.* (Courtesy of Phaidon Press Ltd.)

8. The Aztec earth goddess Cihuacoatl, with mouth agape to show her perpetual hunger for human sacrificial victims. This post-Conquest illustration by an Aztec artist appears in Durán's *Book of the Gods and Rites.* (Redrawn by the author from *"Book of the Gods and Rites" and "The Ancient Calendar,"* by Fray Diego Durán, translated by Horcasitas and Heyden. Copyright © 1971 by the University of Oklahoma Press.)

Preface

THE following attempts to sketch, in a broad and admittedly hasty manner, the story of Mesoamerican civilization from the perspective of that region's changing understandings of the human soul. The native peoples of Ancient America have left behind them an extraordinarily rich legacy of thought on this subject, the serious study of which can yield great rewards to those with the patience and desire to authentically enter the framework of myth and ritual in which this thought is couched. In the century or so since Indian beliefs have begun to be respected for their depth of insight into the human condition, a vast library of secondary literature on the subject has grown up: a body of work that contains a number of masterpieces but which, because of the complexity of the divergent views it presents, can overwhelm a reader seeking a path of entrance into it. As the truth of Jerome Rothenberg's adage that "primitive means complex" has gradually come to be realized, the once ingenuous habits and teachings of our predecessors on the American continent (as well as those of primitive peoples elsewhere) have for some taken on a stigma exactly the opposite of that which they had previously suffered under: these ways of telling have fallen under the cult of specialization, now supposedly demanding years of graduate study before they can be fully read and appreciated—much less written about.

In Mesoamerica—that portion of the continent stretching roughly from the southwestern border of the U.S. down into El Salvador, which during the first millennium of our era saw the rise and fall of innumerable urban centers—this intimidating situation is even worse. Working out the fine points of the kaleidoscopic universes of peoples like the Maya and the Aztecs focused on in this book from the scanty evidence they left behind has proved a daunting task for even the most vigorously studied of scholars, and many of the more substantial works on the topic of necessity read like technical manuals for some monstrous machine whose parts are mostly missing and whose ultimate function is unknown.

The pantheons of each culture were enormous and subject to variation at each particular site. The better known gods have, in addition, the maddening tendency to shift constantly into another. Like characters in a huge, disorganized costume drama, these deities were forever lending their trappings and characteristics to each other, and with each change of costume came a new, multisyllabic name for future scholars to contend with. Quetzalcoatl, the Plumed or Feathered Serpent of the Aztecs, could be variously envisioned as one of several celestial dragons, animalistic god-avatars, or dimly historical human personages, all of these manifestations lacking any immediately discernible similarities in terms of character or function. And this describes the problems of interpretation just within the boundaries of Aztec culture—a boundary within which Quetzalcoatl certainly did not remain. Follow the permutations of this god-complex back into the hazy realms of his birth—among the Maya, the Olmecs, and perhaps even before—and the difficulty of arriving at a clear conception of just this one, comparatively well-documented god, becomes apparent.

Thus books on Mesoamerican religion tend to be either alarmingly complex or suspiciously simple, depending on whether the writer is impelled to stick to the known facts or to yield to the temptations of imagination, letting it take over where the wreckage of the data proves insufficient to make for a good story. In the face of all of these depressing obstacles, I have sought to provide an entrance into Mesoamerican religious ideas by describing some aspects of what for the American of times past was an extremely pressing problem: the nature and destiny of the human soul and its relationship to the natural and supernatural landscapes through which it was thought to move. Though at times I felt overwhelmed by the sheer amount of materials—both original and secondary— that deal with this subject, I was spurred on by the belief that beneath all the academic debates on the origins and attributes of this or that god or rite lay a set of fundamental ideas whose tremendous immediacy and vitality deserved reformulation. The ancient Mesoamericans chose to express themselves complexly, but the questions they chose most often to ask themselves were simple and direct: Why are men and women born and why do they die? Is the human personality eclipsed at death or does it continue somehow, in a world that lies beyond the scope of the naked eye? If human life does not end with the death of the body, what strategies should mortals take in response to this fact?

It may strike those readers with some knowledge of Maya and Aztec religious ideas that of all the varied yet subtly interrelated native American peoples, these two are particularly curious candidates for a book about conceptions of the soul. This would seem to be especially true for the Aztecs, whose knowledge of and interest in the lore of the disembodied soul is considered to have been especially weak in comparison to other ancient American peoples. For reasons that will become apparent in the course of the book, it is my opinion that the builders of Mesoamerica's cities were involved in a constant dialogue with death, that the question of human mortality haunted them to the degree that it had a part to play in each of their creations, be it a statue or a city or a system of government, and that in those times when it seemed least to be in the picture, the problem of the soul's existence after death in fact loomed largest.

In choosing to tell the story of these cities with the specter of human mortality ever in mind, I created a framework with which to sort out the mass of information that scholars of the past hundred years or so have made accessible. In addition to choosing those details which most strongly support my argument, I have tried as well to give the reader unfamiliar with the Mesoamerican universe a taste of it at its most bizarre, humorous, and profound. This material is woven into what in some respects is a historical narrative and what in another respect is itself a kind of myth. Historical writing is always mythmaking to a greater or lesser degree, particularly when the subject is as distant and ambiguous a one as mine. I plead guilty ahead of time to charges of artistic license, and offer in my defense only that I have tried the best I could to distinguish the "hard facts" from my own woolly musings on them. Whatever its shortcomings, I hope the following will at least help to show some of the lesser known sides of these peoples to a wider audience, for there is a great deal that we inheritors of the continent can learn from them.

Acknowledgments

GOOD poets, said T. S. Eliot, don't borrow, they steal. This may be so, but what about good nonfiction writers? The materials used in this book were gathered and pounded into a shape intelligible to the modern reader by a number of experts in American Indian culture—archaeologists, ethnologists, historians, and others—whose ideas on their essential meaning have been incorporated into my own reading of the ancient Mesoamerican world. The notes indicate those places where my borrowing is particularly heavy, but I would like to mention here my indebtedness to several writers in particular without whose works this book would never have found the shape it has.

For the sections on the Aztecs, I am particularly grateful for the works of Burr Cartwright Brundage, which bring the Aztec universe to life while at the same time supplying a conveniently organized catalog of its specific beliefs and practices. My understanding of the Huichol universe is due almost entirely to the writings of Peter T. Furst and Barbara G. Myerhoff, while my reading of the *Popol Vuh* would have been impossible without the recent translation of Dennis Tedlock. John Bierhorst's translations of and commentaries on American Indian songs, myths, and legends have played a large part in the development of my very modest understanding of this world, and this book's debt to those works is evidenced by its many quotations from them. Linda Schele and Mary Ellen Miller's controversial writings on life in the Maya cities helped me develop the original slant of my argument, and their readings of situations depicted in Maya sculpture are the basis for several passages in the first chapter.

Finally, I wish to thank my parents for assistance and encouragement throughout the writing of this book—particularly my father, who struggled to remain calm in the face of my assertions that the Maya's ancestors came to America neither from Atlantis nor Lumeria, but via that tedious land bridge that connected America to Siberia thousands of years ago.

Chronology

c. 1500 B.C.	Beginnings of Olmec civilization on the Gulf Coast.
c. 100 B.C.–A.D. 100	Decline of specifically Olmec civilization. Construction of the first Maya urban centers in jungle lowlands and of Teotihuacan in central Mexico. (Archaeological investigations currently underway may soon push the dates for the first Maya cities back a good deal further.)
23 October 681	Equivalent of Maya date inscribed on Yaxchilán lintel depicting Lady Xoc confronting hallucinatory vision serpent.
31 August 683	Equivalent of Maya date inscribed on sarcophagus lid in Temple of the Inscriptions at Palenque to commemorate King Pacal's death.
c. 650	Fall of Teotihuacan.
c. 800–900	Widespread collapse of great Maya centers.
c. 800–1150	Period of Toltec predominance, centered around Tula.
c. 1150–1350	Gradual descent of Chichimec peoples (future Aztecs, possibly future Huichols) out of northern deserts following the fall of Tula.
1369	Founding of Mexico-Tenochtitlan.
1455	Dedication of Huitzilopochtli's temple at Tenochtitlan.
1503	Montezuma II installed as ruler of Mexico-Tenochtitlan.
21 April 1519	Arrival of Cortez on Gulf Coast.
31 May–13 August 1521	Siege of Mexico. Final defeat of Mexico-Tenochtitlan by Cortez.

I

House of the Four Directions

▼▼▼

In former times the soul was feathered all over.

Plato
Phaedra

THERE IS LITTLE in a pyramid that speaks to us with intimacy. The spare, insistent geometry of some of the better known Egyptian versions may appear to anticipate twentieth-century architecture, but the pyramids of Mesoamerica call up no such familiar associations. Crowded with elaborate stairways and platforms, with the grinning heads of animal-faced gods and the swirling forms of serpents, these structures seem to declare their membership in a world unbridgeably distant from our own.

Today a subtle awkwardness permeates the ancient cities of Palenque and Tikal, Chichen Itza and Teotihuacan. Tourists take photos of gaping, feathered serpent heads, or climb tentatively up shallow stone stairways to the summits, hundreds of feet in the air, of structures that took a staggering investment of time and human resources to create. Witnessing the wreckage of such an intense concentration of human effort creates a desire in the modern observer to share in the lost and perhaps enviable compulsions that came to produce it: yet on any given day at the top of one of the more monstrously proportioned pyramids, the absence of that connection is palpable. Catching one's breath with a handful of fellow outsiders, it is easy to feel the distance, both in time and sensibility, that lies between the realities of the modern world and those that existed on the American continent in the times, now half a millennium in the past, when the building of these artificial mountains was commonplace.

No one knows for certain how the pyramid came to take shape in the Americas. The earliest known example, in the Olmec center of La Venta on the Gulf Coast, is not a pyramid proper but a flat-topped, cone-shaped monument, thirty-four meters high, with a rough series of grooves cut into its sides. The Olmecs developed into Mesoamerica's first "high" culture over a period of about eight hundred years, beginning around 1500 B.C. and fading out before the time of Christ. Pyramidal structures, and grand architectural monuments in general, do not appear to have played as big a part in Olmec life as they did in the civilizations that came after them. The Olmec artist was more interested in creating sculpture than architecture—in particular, sculpture of gods with half-human/half-animal features. Many such works have survived, from delicate jade carvings to massive basalt sculptures weighing thousands of pounds, but the names and functions of the beings they represent are lost. Animalistic features inform so many of the human figures left behind by them that one is tempted to think of the Olmecs as a race of changelings—snake-eyed, jaguar-mouthed protohumans molded by the gods before they had decided on the final appearance that humans and animals were to take in the newly created world. No doubt the Olmecs would have been pleased with this impression, for no matter what the specific social and political characteristics of their probably quite crowded cities were, it is clear that they sought to ally themselves closely with the nations of fish, beasts, and reptiles with whom they shared their jungle habitat.

Believed by most authorities to have been the originators of both the Mesoamerican calendar and the first hieroglyphic writing system, the Olmecs passed much of this cultural inheritance on to the Maya who, along with the mysterious creators of Teotihuacan in the north, brought Mesoamerican culture to its apex of creativity between the fourth and ninth centuries of our era.[1] Recent discoveries in the jungles of northern Guatemala suggest that the classic Maya city may have developed as early as 600 B.C., and with each passing day the picture of the Olmec-Maya relationship takes on new dimensions. By the time this book has gone to press, Maya civilization may have been conclusively proved to be much older than is presently believed. Yet whatever dates are ultimately arrived at, it is likely that the character of Maya civilization will still be understood to have been essentially based on an Olmec model.

Mesoamerica holds within its borders an enormous array of ecological environments, from snow-capped mountains to harsh scrub deserts to tropical jungles. From the coastal swamplands of the Olmecs, the basics of the Mesoamerican urban lifestyle spread inland across this varied terrain over the centuries of the first millennium of our era. The essential uniformity which that lifestyle achieved across the sweep of Mesoamerica during that time has led to speculation that it could not have done so without help from beyond Mesoamerica's shores. The numerous similarities between Old World and New World art and architecture have fueled a continuing debate that Old World incursions had originally spawned the Mesoamerican genius—a debate that sometimes seems more interesting to those involved in it than the deeper meanings of the symbols and structures being discussed. Orthodox scholarship tends overall to deny the possibility of ancient intercontinental contact (or dissemination, as it is called), while a mixed bag of detractors continues to argue, with varying degrees of success, that the Olmecs and the Maya must have received their ideas from an outside source.

Scholars are often fiercely criticized by the more romantic interpreters of Mesoamerican culture for their refusal to believe that one or another ancient people—the Phoenicians, the Egyptians, the Chinese, or others—might have been capable of regularly maneuvering their fragile crafts across the treacherous expanses of ocean separating the Americas from the rest of the civilized world. When arguments of oceanic travel fail, lost continents like Atlantis or Lumeria are brought in to act as sunken stepping-stones for these proposed contacts; and when these will not suffice there is always outer space to turn to.

What is strange about all these bizarre claims is that the most outrageous explanation of the roots of Mesoamerican cultural development is really that one agreed upon by the cautious world of conventional archaeology. For if, as seems most likely, the peoples of Mesoamerica were descended solely from hunter-gatherers who moved down from Siberia across the land bridge that once connected the Americas to the Old World, and if that Ice Age crossing was the last true contact between the Old and the New Worlds until the time of the Vikings, then the very particular shape of the pyramid, and the inclination to bring that shape into being on an enormous scale, must be understood to have occurred spontaneously in the minds of two or more widely separated peoples. Above and beyond Atlantis, Lumeria, or the Egypt of the Pharaohs, the landscape of the human psyche itself is surely the most interesting and provocative of the pyramid's many stated lands of origin.

The question of diffusion is only the first of many which the pyramid and its American creators conjure up. Since 1841, when Frederick Catherwood and John Lloyd Stephens began publishing

2. Detail by Catherwood of ruins at the Maya city of Tulum on the Yucatan coast.

the first detailed accounts of the area and the ruined cities that lay scattered across it, the details of life in ancient Middle America have generated a tremendous amount of argument among scholars, artists, and self-styled cultural exegetes of every description. Catherwood produced a series of elegant illustrations of these cities that whetted the curiosity of nineteenth-century Europe, while Stephens provided an accompanying text of thoughtful speculations on the character of the peoples who produced them.

Since then the speculation, both thoughtful and otherwise, has continued unabated, most of it focusing on the great Maya centers of the Yucatan and lowland Guatemala. Up until now almost all of the more outlandish theories about ancient Mesoamerican civilization have been aimed at the Maya, primarily because a convenient absence of verifiable information on their vast and gracefully constructed cities allowed writers to say whatever they liked about them without fear of proof to the contrary. Almost nothing was known about ancient Maya society until very recently, whereas entirely too much was known about their successors, the Aztecs: details of their horrendously bloody religious rituals, taken down by Spanish friars from native informants in the years after the Conquest, have made them both the most verifiably documented, and the least liked, of all the Mesoamerican civilizations.

No such accounts exist about the Maya. Most of their cities had lain dormant for more than five hundred years by the time of the Spaniards' arrival. The Conquistadors passed by many of these cities unawares, and were not much interested in those they did notice, the accumulation of gold and Christian souls taking precedence over archaeological curiosity. The largest and most reliable source of information on the ancient Maya was and is the fabulously ornate series of hieroglyphic inscriptions that cover the surfaces of their temples, stelae, and pyramids, and until very recently these glyphs were a closed language. Without an understanding of these hermetic glyphs the Maya were fair game for a huge spectrum of conflicting opinion.

But this era of wild speculation is coming to an end. Until recently, the consensus on Maya civilization was that it was generally a peaceful theocracy whose gargantuan architectural productions were inspired by an innocent, abstract wonder at the movements of the celestial bodies. Recent breakthroughs in glyph decipherment, which began in the fifties and have been accelerating steadily ever since, have conclusively abolished this long-

3. A Maya battle scene from the eighth century A.D. *The smaller figures at center are rival warriors being taken captive.*

standing view. These breakthroughs give Maya civilization a new and unexpectedly sinister cast and have made it extremely difficult to place them above and beyond their supposedly more blood-thirsty successors. Many of the human figures depicted in stone by Maya artists are now believed to have been not benign celestial priests but severe kings, queens, and princes, who upheld authority and guarded their status as brutally as any in the long and violent history of humankind.

These new developments have not been borne with equanimity by the majority of Maya enthusiasts. Linda Schele and Mary Ellen Miller, authors of a groundbreaking synthesis of these new discoveries, have remarked that

> as this new understanding of the Maya has emerged over the
> past twenty-five years, many people have been repulsed by con-

vincing evidence of human sacrifice and blood offerings and have drawn away from such a tangible or realistic view of the Maya. In Mesoamerican studies, a propensity for gore had always been attributed to the Aztecs. In contrast, the Maya were always assumed to be a superior race, thoroughly removed in time, space and culture from such behavior. In the new view ... they have fallen from their pedestal; in doing so, they become a part of the community of man, the builders of a civilization that included both the darkest and the most brilliant possibilities of human behavior.[2]

Since the publication of their book *The Blood of Kings* in 1986, Schele and Miller have incurred a great deal of wrath as well as praise for their pronouncements. Their evidence is so convincing that some authors, intent on believing that Maya civilization embodied a lost wisdom untainted by the uglier aspects of primitive cultures, have chosen to ignore it altogether. The fury of this denial says interesting things about twentieth-century humankind's view of itself. If ancient societies are only valuable as Rorschach blots on which to project our own fantasies without regard for the inevitable failings of our all-too-human predecessors on the planet, and if we lose interest in those societies once it is discovered that life in them was just as complex and rife with paradox as is our own, then we stand little chance of gaining an understanding, more pressing in this century than ever before, of those "darkest and most brilliant possibilities," which we still very far from godlike humans might yet contain.

It is possible that as the results of the new readings of Maya glyphs become more widely known, and these peoples come more and more to resemble the civilizations that came before and after them on the American continent, the amount of popular books written on the Maya will slacken off, and other civilizations, less preoccupied with the troublesome business of sacrifice and bloodletting, will take their place in the public imagination. This would be unfortunate, for within the confusing and often repugnant history of the Maya and their neighbors there lies the outline of a secret narrative as bizarre and interesting as any concocted by these peoples' more unconventional interpreters. This narrative can only come to make sense to us when we adopt a form of perception that our civilized ancestors abandoned hundreds of years ago—a perception that we can refer to by the convenient if somewhat stigmatized term "animism": the belief in, and experience of, the world as a living entity whose every object, material or otherwise, contains a force and personality of its own. Everything that we have come to understand about the builders of Mesoamerica's first metropolitan communities indicates that they lived in a universe pervasively alive from top to bottom, and when the architecture of those cities is examined with this style of perception in mind, their design can be seen to specifically reflect and address this condition of aliveness.

There appears to have been no arbitrarily placed pyramid in Mesoamerica; each face was constructed in reference to one of four cardinal points in space—the same ones we know as north, south, east, and west. In our world these directions tend to function as convenient reference points but little more. We use them as relative designations, knowing that if we headed south long enough we would circle the globe and end up where we started. The ancient Mesoamerican did not think in such terms. For him or her, physical and psychological space, the outer and inner worlds, were not distinctly separable, and everything in the outer world, including something as seemingly vague as a direction, could be seen as an autonomous being that monitored the human community with watchful eyes.

The same preoccupation with direction existed elsewhere in the ancient world. Eden had four gates, and four rivers leading out of it. In Mesopotamia and the first cities of Asia, Europe, and Africa, the city was conceived as a quadripartite realm whose structure mirrored that of heaven. Regardless of how the questions of contact between pre-Columbian America and the Old World are resolved, the persistent uniformity of the world's first cities has been partially explained as resulting from the uniformity of the human body and the ways in which it naturally experiences itself as meaningfully oriented in space. It has been argued that humans tend to live in quadripartite cities because they are by nature quadripartite creatures: beings whose structure is oriented along a central axis (the spine) and divided into two parallel halves (feet, legs, hands, eyes, etc.). In this view, each individual is a city in him- or herself—an ambivalent and yet perpetual center that naturally apprehends the world around it in terms of front or back, right or left. The ordered movements of certain external features of the universe, primarily that of the sun across the sky, encourage humankind to cast this natural division outwards, thus initiating the fourfold mapping of the cosmos so universally apparent in the shape of the world's villages and cities.

Throughout Mexico and Guatemala, as well as in the bordering Indian regions of the American Southwest, the four directions were held in particularly great esteem. The Maya believed that in each direction stood a deity called a Bacab, a mythological being responsible for supporting his particular quadrant of the cosmos. The sky stood above the earth thanks to these creatures, and numerous ritual devotions were offered to them in order to sustain and reward their efforts on behalf of humankind. The Aztecs believed that each direction had a "personality" of its own, which manifested particular aspects of the journey of human life. East, the direction where the sun emerges each day from the bowels of the underworld, was characterized as the direction of youth and potency. From there a person moved south into adulthood and west into old age, the direction of the sun's daily fall back into the underworld. North was the direction of death and decay. To face or travel north had grave implications, for it was there that a soul could lose itself forever and not be able to return back to the east, which often served as a fifth as well as first direction—the place not only of birth but of rebirth.[3]

The Mesoamerican pyramid served not only to mark these cardinal points and the life journey they represented, but also, through its existence in physical space with them, allowed its makers to enter into communication with the four quarters and the aspects of human destiny they contained. Time and space thus blended magically together to form a single element in which the soul played out its fate.

But the fate of humankind did not end at death, and so the cosmic stage on which the human drama was enacted did not stop at the terrestrial plane. The four quarters were thought to lie at the midpoint of a many-leveled cosmos that stretched down into a fearful region of hells and up into a glorious celestial realm, which the pyramidal structure, standing at the midpoint of both vertical and horizontal space, addressed as well. A pyramid could have nine tiers because heaven possessed nine levels; it could have 365 steps leading to the summit because the year possessed 365 days, each of which had a personality and temperament of its own. There was no detail of the Mesoamerican universe that did not bode either ill or well, and the pyramid served as a kind of index to the complicated natural ciphers that the universe offered to men and women as a puzzle to unravel. Because substance and symbol did not live apart in this thoughtfully constructed arena of meanings, because to name or represent a god or an object was essentially to conjure up the force of its presence, the pyramid did not just mirror the structure of the cosmos but brought its energies into a focus point of incredible power. To live in a sacred city was to live close to the borderline between life and death, between the "middle world" of living humans and the multileveled realms existing above and beneath it.

The power center for a living sacred city like Tikal or Chichen Itza was the pyramid, for through it such cities enjoyed communication with the spectrum of worlds that made up the universe, of which the human community itself was but a thin wedge. In these times a city's kings and queens could command great wealth, but their success or failure as rulers depended on their ability to engage the world around them in a meaningful dialogue that brought the energies within and behind that universe into the human sphere.

We fool ourselves when we call such ancient societies "pure" and our own "corrupt," if all we are measuring these terms by is degrees of fascination with wealth. Ancient civilizations were as transfixed by the finery and power of the upper classes as is our own, the difference being that in those times ostentation had supernatural reference points we choose no longer to acknowledge. Several post-Freudian theorists have demonstrated how, in our society, excessive accumulation of wealth can be seen as a disguised longing for immortality. In ancient Mesoamerica this longing was not disguised, and a king or a great warrior was envied because the riches and abilities he possessed indicated familiarity with the landscapes and situations that awaited mortals at death.

Modern society pretends to have left it behind, but this type of overt preoccupation with the afterlife is one of the most consistent trademarks of our ancient heritage, found everywhere, with minor variations, throughout the surviving native communities who have kept alive into the present day spiritual traditions that began in the Stone Age. Among these primitive communities one figure—known as a shaman after a Siberian term, thought originally to signify something like "one who burns"—tends to fill the role of spiritual emissary between the human and transhuman planes.

In the past hundred years the art of shamanizing has been described and catalogued by researchers and explorers on every continent. The results of all this observation were first presented in a truly coherent fashion by Mircea Eliade, the great historian of religions, in his *Shamanism: Archaic Techniques of Ecstasy*, which first appeared in France in 1951. Eliade describes the shaman as a being set apart from others by his skills in ecstatic travel (in the word's original connotation of release from the stasis of physical embodiment). This figure's ability to travel beyond the limits of normal human experience is attained through an eccentric but extremely widespread series of experiences that usually begin with a prolonged initiatory ordeal occurring around puberty. In primitive tribes from Australia to Alaska, certain young men (or women, though this is generally less common) are noticed by their elders to become dreamy and distracted, singing to themselves, walking into things, and otherwise demonstrating a significant lack of involvement with the more mundane concerns of tribal life. This is taken as a sign that the supernaturals have singled the youth out as a potential shaman, and preparations are then made for his or her transformation into a full-fledged representative of the forces and energies lying outside the strictly human domain.

These initiations are often physically and psychologically dangerous. The youth is forced to spend long periods in isolation, with little food or shelter. Fear and fatigue wear at him; in visions brought on by hunger and exhaustion, the neophyte enters a kind of psychotic state in which, lying comatose on the floor of a simple shelter or alone in the deserted forests or fields beyond the village, he experiences the sensation of being torn to pieces by the gods of the universe, most especially those whose province is disease and death. These gods might devour him whole, holding him within their stomachs until he is nothing but a skeleton. In a variation on this motif, the severed pieces of his body might be cooked in a great cauldron. Eliade examined numerous such scenarios and arrived at the conclusion that these initiations were often enactments on a mythological level of a genuine rending and reintegration of the human psyche. If the potential shaman is not driven permanently insane by his ordeal, he returns to human society with increased strength of both body and spirit. Having been torn apart and "rebuilt" by the forces of the other world, he is no longer just a man, but a dual being who is no longer afraid of death because he has experienced its mysteries and survived them.

Throughout their careers, shamans serve their community by undergoing ecstatic states in which the soul departs from the body to converse with the souls of the dead and the gods of weather and disease, death and fertility. By keeping up appearances with these entities, shamans safeguard their people from the dangers of hunger and disease and let them know what to expect from the divinities of the surrounding natural world. As important as these practical ends may be to the other members of the village (and there is plentiful documentation of such feats, many of them as yet unexplained), an equally important service is provided by the accompanying worldview these endeavors encourage. Largely thanks to the shaman, an unassuming collection of huts can become a weigh station for gods and ancestral spirits of every description. Genuine shamanic communities do not just believe abstractly in the essential "animistic" tenets of the soul's independence of the body and the network of spiritual energies with which the natural landscape receives it: they experience them as day-to-day realities. After he or she has mastered in solitude the techniques of otherworldly travel, the shaman will usually conduct his or her ecstatic voyages in public, before the assembled villagers. Watching the entranced shaman's alien cries and contortions, these people take part in a dialogue between their world and another one, which their limited, merely human stature does not allow them to enter but which they can nevertheless experience at a slight remove through the efforts of this talented intermediary.

The shamanic experience lies at an earlier level of cultural development than the societies of Mesoamerica's pyramidal cities. Here the shaman was replaced by the kings, queens, and high priests who current researchers insist were so disturbingly preoccupied with material manifestations of power such as war, bloodletting, and sacrifice. But what is most fascinating and suggestive in the new readings of peoples like the ancient Maya is the iconographic background of these rites of violence. The scenarios and the language of these rituals are full of shamanic motifs, and if we manage to get past their surface violence, we find that they are referring to the same kind of out-of-body voyage that the shamanic tradition spent so many hundreds of years developing. A great king might be shown at the moment of death, as on the sarcophagus lid of the famous Temple of the Inscriptions at Palenque. This lid resided in a pyramid, and it covered the body of a king named Pacal, who on the lid itself is represented at the moment of his entrance into the underworld. The highly stylized imagery surrounding the figure of the king on this relief has led to speculations by some of Maya civilization's less orthodox inter-preters that he is at the controls of a magnificent space capsule. Conventional scholarship pays little attention to this theory, but the analogy to our modern mechanical world is actually astute. Like an astronaut, this man is involved in a prodigious journey between worlds: the same one undertaken by the shaman, whose prestige in the eyes of society he has inherited.

The king Pacal is shown seated upon a wild-eyed deity known to scholars as the Quadripartite Monster. This beast represents the sun, whose trajectory into the underworld at sunset and trium-phantly back into the sky at dawn the deceased king is supposed to follow. The main body of the "space capsule" is actually a very highly stylized version of the world tree, or *axis mundi*, which throughout history has been a remarkably popular symbol of the avenue of travel and communication between the worlds of the living and the dead. This tree represents the same axis point which the pyramid itself makes manifest: Pacal's soul will spin down it into the sepulchral, multileveled Maya underworld of Xibalba, or "Place of Fear," a realm inhabited by a host of spooks and demons in various stages of scarifying decay. The ancient Maya were both terrified and fascinated by this realm. From it issued disease, drought, and generally all the conditions that made humans' lot in life a difficult one. Plunging into this world of living nightmare, the freshly departed soul struggled to keep its bearings, fending off the attacking spirits that sought to confuse it and rob it of its potency. These spirits were strong but not invincible: a soul that had built up its strength in the period of its earthly incarnation might suc-cessfully fend them off and find its way to the celestial paradise at the crown of the "tree" of the universe (also represented on Pacal's tomb lid), the crystalline splendor of which was hinted at in the finery that surrounded the king on earth.

Thus the tomb, and the pyramid in which it was sealed, served both map and roadway for an intricate spiritual journey whose details were first intuited by the Maya's shamanic ancestors in periods of sleep and trance. A pyramid holding a dead king was testimony of a journey taken along perilous pathways of the uni-verse, by a man whose greatness and spiritual potency the people hoped to emulate. Just as the stars knew their way across the night sky, this man would presumably find his way through the crowded night-world beneath the earth, and in doing so succeed in joining their company as a body of light in the world above. Such a suc-

4. Pacal's tomb-lid featuring the world tree with celestial bird at the top and the gaping, stylized jaws of the underworld at bottom.

cessful navigation demonstrated the soul's reality and its place in the universe—a universe that did not stop at the limits of the physical world but continued beyond it, just as the fate of the individual soul did not stop at death but to a degree began there.

Much of that area of the mind we have come to call the subconscious was, for the spiritual mapmakers of ancient America, subterranean. By allowing the hallucinatory landscape of dream a status alongside that of the physical world itself, these peoples created for themselves from the known world of rocks, rivers, and sky, a precarious dwelling place set about with openings into the world of disincarnate spirits.

It is no wonder then that the cave in Middle America was a primary sacred space. The Aztecs believed themselves to have come originally from a "Place of Seven Caves," and the enormous Pyramid of the Sun, the largest and earliest sacred structure at Teotihuacan in central Mexico, is centered directly upon a natural cave that the city's creators enlarged into a clover-shaped space before building the pyramid over it. Other openings—grottoes, lakes, and cenotes—were equally revered as passage points to the beyond. A large natural cenote at Chichen Itza was important not only as a source of water, which in the Yucatan is quite scarce aboveground, but as a reception point for sacrificial victims. The riverine world of the lowland Classic Maya in Guatemala, whose dark waterways supported large fish and reptile populations, provided the peoples of this area with an abundant food source and a constant reminder of the closeness at hand of the spirit world.[4]

Over and above these natural entrances, what made the pyramid such a special entryway into the beyond was its specifically structured orientation. A pyramid was evidence that the people who built it knew exactly where they stood within the contiguous universes of life and death. Mesoamerica shared with other ancient cultures a belief that the shock of death could confer a dangerous forgetfulness upon the newly disembodied spirit. Like those cultures it possessed an extensive body of instructive material to be learned in life for use afterwards, for it was believed that success in the afterworld depended on a strong foreknowledge of the specific nature of the lands that the soul was destined to enter at death. Without it, one was doomed to wander through these regions like a drunkard in a strange and dangerous town, reeling into quarters best stayed out of, talking to persons best left alone. Because a pyramid was a centralized locus of the cosmos—indeed, many of the great Mesoamerican centers considered themselves, at the height of their influence, as lying at the center of the world—to descend along its axis brought one into the underworld armed against disorientation.

▲▲▲▲▲▲▲
▼▼▼▼▼▼▼

This structured style of underworld entry had a long tradition in Mesoamerica. The rugged terrain of western Mexico supports, even to this day, a community known as the Huichols who share the Mesoamerican legacy of the shaman but who never moved beyond the first stages of village life that their neighbors to the southeast abandoned over two thousand years ago. Limited food resources, distance from centers of cultural activity, and the native temperament of these peoples have combined to keep them at a simpler level of development, making them an excellent source of information on the primitive roots of the higher civilizations to which they are closely related. Small family communities live together in primitive mini-villages thought to be similar to those that might have existed in pre-Olmec times. Numbering as few as fifteen individuals, these scattered groups live in close communion with their ancestors, who are believed to live in a pleasant and unassuming underworld where life goes on much as it does for the living. (Though without, as Peter T. Furst, a specialist in this area puts it, "some of the more onerous aspects of earthly life. Since the mortality rate among children is high, such sexual intercourse as there may be in the underworld is said not to lead to pregnancy.")[5]

The religious life of these peoples is characterized by a likable simplicity that accepts the natural and supernatural worlds as twin poles of a cosmic unity encompassing both. The dead hold festive dances and sometimes sneak back into the world of the living to partake of the ceremonial maize beer of which both the living and the dead, according to Furst, are extremely fond. The earth exists for these peoples as an island afloat in a sea of spiritual force that is capable of invading and informing each aspect of physical existence. It is a world at once stranger and less lonely than our own, where one direction is much the same as the next, and death is an abstraction for which the landscape holds no landmarks. The ceremonial huts, or *xirikis*, of these communities are oriented toward the four directions in the same manner as the sacred structures of the great Mesoamerican centers. Such huts are designated as special by their rectangular shape, and function as residences of ancestral shamans—disembodied spirits who after their death have been coaxed through prolonged ceremonial efforts to enter into tiny, uncut quartz crystals that are then attached to ceremonial arrows and lodged in the roof of the house, which in this case is conical. From this hut a living shaman, taking strength from the numen lodged in the arrow, can travel to the underworld in spirit form to converse with the dead. It is an orienting communication point between worlds and the predecessor, in more ways than one, of Palenque's Temple of the Inscriptions, where the evidence of the soul-potency of the king Pacal resided, not in the form of an uncut rock crystal tied to an arrow, but as a physical body immured in a tomb inscribed with what appears to us at first as the control center of an impressive rocket ship.

From hut to pyramid, the history of Mesoamerican civilization revolved around an ancient legacy of spiritual travel, the details of which were surprisingly similar given the political and economic differences that separate a Huichol village from a Maya metropolis. It seems obvious that such a unified concern could not have survived so long, undergoing so many changes yet remaining so much the same, if it had not been based on potent spiritual or psychological experiences. Through the adventures of a talented spiritual aristocracy of priests and kings, and before them of shamans, these experiences were used to create an interplay of mundane and supernatural concerns that when successful made life and death intensely dependent on one another. The importance of this interdependence between spirit and flesh is illustrated by a remarkable folkloric fragment from the villages of the Huichols. Again according to Furst, the soul of the deceased, when setting out for the villages of the dead, is believed to be obligated to take along, in a sack slung over its shoulder, the sexual organs of all the partners with which he or she had coupled during life.

> At various points along the way the soul, increasingly tired and hungry and eager to reach its destination, attempts more or less surreptitiously to rid itself of the burden, but the ancestors and

the owners of the underworld will not permit this: 'you wanted to enjoy yourself in that other life,' they call out to the relative, 'now you must carry all of that on your back to arrive here.'[6]

Arriving after a long and eventful journey at the dancing ground where he or she will be welcomed festively by a crowd of deceased relatives, the newly dead soul sets down the sack beneath an enormous fig tree, which Furst identifies with the cosmic world-axis. This tree is full of ripe fruits that are to be collected by the neophyte spirit, who knocks them down by throwing his or her collected vaginas or penises up into the branches. Thereupon a great feast is prepared, and "all the people there are happy for their relative has brought them life."[7]

This inspired little story conceals a profound belief that human (for lack of a better term) "energy" is needed by the divine world as much as divine energy is needed by the human. To bring sexual energy into the world of death is to a certain degree equivalent to bringing life itself there. To be dead while alive, and alive while dead, is one of the primary feats of the primitive spiritual traveler. By mastering this capacity he or she obtains that greatest of all autonomies: the power to survive death as a discrete, personified spiritual entity. Whether the underworld was portrayed as a cheerful picnic ground or a treacherous realm of demons, as it tended to be for all the more advanced cultures, the same insistence on communication and reciprocal exchange of goods was always stressed; it was this that gave the individual soul the power to maintain its integrity after the supportive web of physicality had fallen away.

Reciprocity was important for the gods as well as for mortals. The *Popol Vuh*, the epic of the Quiche Maya people and the greatest single nonhieroglyphic repository of details concerning life in the Classic Maya universe, insists that the gods first made men and women in order that they would have someone to address them in prayer and ritual. This mythic narrative states that the gods created three races of beings before arriving at the humans of today. The first race, from whom the animals of today are descended, were unsatisfactory because they were incapable of addressing their creators with meaningful words. A second effort yielded a creature of mud who again failed to satisfy the gods, and a third try resulted in an extremely disrespectful race of wooden mannequins: "They came into being, they multiplied, they had daughters, they had sons. . . . But there was nothing in their hearts and nothing in their minds, no memory of their mason and builder. They just went and walked wherever they wanted."[8] For this disrespect a catastrophe was brought down upon them and the gods tried one more time, producing at last a race of beings capable of carrying out the complex and vital discourse between worlds: a discourse for which the gods hungered as much as humans.

As a coherent center of communication with the world beyond the ordinary senses, the pyramid not only opened the earth for the human spirit's travel downwards, but at certain times and under certain conditions allowed for the controlled emergence into the day-world of celestial and chthonic personalities. The Classic Maya recorded some of these encounters in stone. On a series of lintels at the center of Yaxchilán in Chiapas, two moments in this process of evocation and communication are vividly portrayed. In the first a woman named Lady Xoc, the wife of a king that specialists in Maya glyph decipherment know as Shield Jaguar, pulls a thick rope entwined with thorns through a hole in her tongue.[9] The blood from this wound flows into a basket full of paper strips, placed at her knees to absorb the vital fluid. Blood for the Maya was by all indications a supremely potent substance: it was in many ways the currency of the spirit world made manifest. Royal blood ritually drawn contained a tremendous amount of energy—so much that its collection in the pictured basket could rend the membrane between worlds in the same way that a magnifying glass, held over the surface of a brittle leaf on a sunny day, will bring a sudden, smoking hole into being.

Another lintel, again featuring Lady Xoc, records the results of such a bloodletting procedure. From the basket of bloodied strips emerges a twisting, kaleidoscopically intricate serpent. It rises over Lady Xoc like a swirling, demonic genie, its otherworldly nature evidenced by the cacophony of faces and sacred symbols that bristle from each curve of its body. This snake has a head at both ends. From the mouth of each come manifestations of the god this ceremony was apparently intended to reveal—one who scholars suspect was associated with the activities of war, sacrifice, and bloodletting in general.

Like so many of the figures in Maya iconography, this imposing serpent is so complexly rendered that it takes a moment to differentiate it as a discrete entity, and another moment to find any similarities between it and its less flamboyant terrestrial cousins. It is thought that the beings emerging from both ends of the serpent are in fact the same god because of certain identifying glyphs attached to each. Other than that, the face emerging from the lower mouth of the serpent looks nothing like the one emerging from the top. The former is rendered in the same nightmarish, cartoony style as the serpent, but the top figure, who looms in the space above Lady Xoc with a brandished spear, seems to belong to the day-world of normal flesh-and-blood humans.[10]

Maya artists like the one who produced this scene were highly skilled in the realistic representation of people and objects: they did not feel compelled to depict every aspect of their world surrealistically. Thus the cartoony, distorted appearance of some figures and the naturalistic representation of others in the same scene suggest that for these artists the world of dream and the world of everyday reality could sometimes overlap, allowing beings from both realms to meet and converse. There is evidence that in dream, trance, or a visionary stupor induced by hours or even days of ritual dancing and autolaceration, the Maya petitioned the gods to appear before their eyes and in this respect were struggling to remain faithful to the shamanic tradition of visionary ecstasy that had bequeathed to them their peculiar and vivid universe. At its height, the Maya pantheon was not a fondly held abstraction, a bloodless mental arena where supernatural figures pursued human goals on a larger scale (such as did the later, degenerated pantheons of the Greeks and Romans), but an encircling field of transhuman force that could overwhelm the human community at any moment. The intensity of such a world is hard to imagine: it is like living perennially in the first stages of waking consciousness that return after a particularly vivid dream, when for a moment "dream" and "reality" are confused. For us at such times it is just a matter of waiting for the mundane world to gradually return and rescue us from whatever troubling or paradisal scene we had imagined. For the ancient Maya and Aztecs, that certainty never arrived, for they lived in a world where real and unreal were not so easily separated.

5. Lady Xoc, *with the subterranean vision serpent rising before her.*

The great Classic Maya cities were miracles of architectural and economic organization. Breakthroughs in food production and distribution, trade relations with other cities, and refinements in craft production and the arts of war established an unprecedented standard of empire, which later civilizations strove to emulate. Yet at the heart of Maya civilization there appears to have been some fundamental flaw or contradiction, which in the ninth century of our era caused a monumental collapse from which none of the principal Maya cities escaped. Here as elsewhere with the Maya, there is no definite agreement as to what brought about this sudden decline, but the archaeological record shows that for whatever reason, the energy and cohesion that had powered Maya civilization for eight centuries suddenly and everywhere gave out. Cities that once housed thousands of individuals were left empty, projects in stone were left half-finished, and the people to a large extent reverted to the simpler village societies they had left behind centuries ago.

Detailed economic and political explanations for the collapse have been advanced, blaming it on a breakdown in the local ecology brought about by excessive cultivation of the land, the invasion of hostile peoples from the north, or the revolt of the "masses" against an aristocracy that was pressing them beyond their endurance. No single explanation has been proved, and all may be valid to a greater or lesser degree. But behind all of these material causes might lie an equally significant spiritual one. As it was this people's intense preoccupation with otherworldly matters that supplied much of the all-but-superhuman energy necessary to raise their cities in the midst of dense and unforgiving jungles without the benefit of pack animals and other Old World amenities, it is reasonable to look in that direction for causes of their decline as well.

In every age but our own, the happiness of humanity was understood to depend on access to spiritual as well as material resources; but it has also long been recognized that too much wealth and progress can lead to trouble when it occludes the realities of the spiritual domain to which human beings have always looked for orientation and inspiration. The seriousness of the spiritual difficulties that a vital community can encounter while coping with the changes progress brings has been illustrated countless times in the disastrous encounters between primitive communities and modern civilization that have occurred over the past few hundred years.

Primitive societies are often based on a complex and, to the outsider, largely invisible web of beliefs and values that bind the lives of humans to the forces of nature and the spiritual entities that move behind and through them. A serious tear in this web of interrelated laws and forces can bring a culture's entire belief system into question. Primitive cultures are always compelled to relate the truths of the human spirit to the outside world, and when this divinely saturated world is tampered with, or shown to be radically different from what it was believed to be, the religiously inspired mind struggles to find reasons for the new situation. Hence Cargo Cults and Ghost Dances, and the countless other gropings at explanation of new phenomena that we moderns have often found so amusing and pathetic. If, as is usually the case with modern civilization's encroachments upon traditional societies, the changes come at too rapid and confusing a pace, the world of meaning collapses and what once was a thriving and dynamic community becomes a collection of dead souls, listless and susceptible to whatever new belief system is thrust upon them.

It is often not realized that a primitive civilization can be capable of disorienting itself without help from outside forces. Long before the arrival of Cortez, Mesoamerican civilization had grown materially beyond the boundaries of the religious worldview that the geniuses of this civilization had designed to validate and direct it. Its extravagant cities were based on a model of the universe that had not changed radically in structure since shamanic times. As civilization advanced, and the shaman's hut grew into a temple or pyramid, it perhaps became impossible for the entire population of a city to share in the same intimate experience of divinity that had occurred regularly in the primitive village. The populace would now be told, instead of shown, that the gods existed, and the pyramids and other sacred structures no longer served as entrances into the supernatural realms but acted instead as barriers to them. At length the shamanic model proved incapable of providing that intense communication with the universe in all its aspects that had given the Mesoamerican spirit such strength and vitality to begin with, and disaster ensued.

This scenario would carry no more weight than all the other proposed reasons for the Maya collapse were it not for the fact that the Maya themselves have left us myths and stories that describe its unfolding. The Maya were aware of the dangers and contradictions of human progress and had in fact anticipated the disasters that this progress would come to bring about. From its inception, the rise out of village life was plagued with feelings of guilt and ambiguity—feelings that the Maya expressed in mythological terms.

Inheritors of the Judeo-Christian tradition are familiar enough with the notion that human knowledge entails guilt. Our own preferred mythic compilation tells us that human life fell into its present state when Adam, biting of the apple of knowledge, was exiled with his mate from the paradise of Eden. Strangely enough, it seems that the builders of Mesoamerica's pyramid-cities were plagued with similar feelings of ambiguity about their departure from the four-cornered garden of the primitive village. An atmosphere of guilt pervades Mesoamerican accounts of the founding of cities and the rise to glory of their peoples. There is the persistent implication—present in the myths of many peoples but here consistently associated with the urban advances to which Mesoamerica was so prone—that each step in this departure is an act of potential impertinence that takes humankind further from its original spiritual homeland and the condition of grace that it enjoyed there.

"The guilt is ours!" exclaim the mythic first peoples of the Quiche Maya, whose wanderings are chronicled in the latter half of the *Popol Vuh*. The reasons for this guilt are never stated explicitly in the narrative, but it appears when the first human lineages, walking the world in darkness, converge at a place in the east called Tulan Zuya, or Seven Caves, believed by some to correspond to that original place of caves from which Teotihuacan rose. As such it represents the germination point of the first, and therefore archetypal, city—the primary point of interaction between the human and the divine to which humankind is to look from then on for instructions and information on its place in the cosmos. Under various names, such a locus formed the model for all Mesoamerican cities of consequence, each of which sought to imitate, and thus become, the place itself.[11]

The *Popol Vuh* states that here at the perennial world-center, each lineage was given a god to worship, the most important of whom was called Tohil. This deity is related to, or perhaps the same as, a Classic Maya deity named Tahil, who is pictured at the city of Palenque with the all-important symbol of the smoking mirror on his forehead. The fact of this god's importance for the Quiche narrators of the *Popol Vuh* is significant, for the god of the smoking mirror in the Aztec pantheon, there called Tezcatlipoca, is strongly associated by some scholars with the lost shamanic tradition.

What the *Popol Vuh* might here be narrating, in the veiled manner characteristic of myth, is the ascent of the Mayan peoples into the consciousness of an advanced civilization and the danger of losing communication with the gods involved in this advance. In this predawn world the god Tohil controls the power of fire, which he dispenses to the various tribes on the condition that they will allow him to "suckle" them later on. Fire is a preeminent symbol of human culture: from its mastery everything else eventually follows. Hence in North American mythology a primordial fire theft, accomplished by a variety of Promethean animal characters, is a common theme in the tales of man's development into a cultural being. Here in the *Popol Vuh*, fire is not stolen but given away by the god himself, but on one important and foreboding condition. To be "suckled" by the god means, according to *Popol Vuh* translator Dennis Tedlock, to be sacrificed to him.

The *Popol Vuh* states that with the coming of the first dawn the gods were hardened by the sun's light into static idols no longer able to speak to humans except as spirits. This is one example of an extremely widespread mythological motif equating the birth of human culture with the "drying" or "hardening" of the primordial world that preceded it. Civilization on any level was a dangerous commodity to the primitive mind, but where urban cultures are concerned it became doubly so. We can read this "hardening" of the gods into idols as a suggestion that the light of human understanding is potentially offensive to the spirit world, and with each advance of this understanding, communication with the divine becomes more and more difficult to achieve.

The first tribes converge at the Place of Seven Caves to receive the gift of civilization from the gods, and to learn the consequences of that gift. Later in the story Tohil, through the rock idol that has come to hold his retreated essence, will demand blood of his subjects, and they will be forced to find it for him. Solitary travelers are abducted and sacrificed before the god. At first the other tribes blame wild animals for the mysterious disappearance of their fellows. Soon, however, it is revealed that the followers of Tohil are responsible. In retribution for extracting the first payments for the burden of civilization, Tohil's followers are then set upon by the other tribes. Warfare, as the vehicle of divine sustenance, is born, and the bodies begin to pile up. They continue to do so for the rest of Mesoamerican history: the price paid for humanity's ambiguous advance into higher levels of culture.

Both Maya and Aztec civilization have left us many legends that show the boon of civilization to be a double-edged sword. As the simple shaman's hut grew into a massive pyramid, the relatively simple and easy relation between humans and the divine became a strained and dangerous one, requiring copious amounts of blood to be kept working. In cities like the Maya centers of Palenque and Tikal, and later in the Aztec cities like Tenochtitlan, crowds under the leadership of a complex religious hierarchy engaged in frenzied mass evocations of the gods, who year by year grew more displeased with their human charges. The tragic pattern of meteoric growth followed by catastrophic decline was repeated time and again by city after city in Mesoamerica. Such was the natural course of empire, and most cultures seem to have been aware of it. Why, then, did these cities obstinately keep rising from the ruins of their predecessors? Why did the Aztecs revere the Toltecs, a people whose civilization they believed had ended in disaster because of failure to adhere to divine law? And why were they ready to expect exactly the same fate for themselves—so ready, in fact, that the arrival of the Spaniards was greeted not so much with surprise and anger as with resignation?

It would appear that these societies had arrived at a kind of stalemate in their relations with the divine. Unable to live happily in a universe whose every aspect they did not understand on an immediate and intuitive level, yet unable to halt the momentum of human technical and social advancements that were making these realms harder and harder to stay in contact with, they strove to keep the lines of access to this subtle reservoir of meanings open through the construction of larger and larger pyramids and the sacrifice of more and more human beings. Yet by Aztec times it was clear that the battle was largely lost, that the divine had retreated from the human sphere to a point perhaps beyond recall and was now only peripherally interested in humans as a source of blood. Such an impossible state of affairs could not have been borne forever, and it is likely that had Cortez not shown up when he did, Aztec civilization would either have found other causes for collapse or undergone a massive transformation in terms of its general worldview.

By the fifteenth century of our era, a new strategy for recalling the disenchanted gods into communication with humanity was definitely in order. Humankind had spent the vast majority of its time on this planet as wanderers or simple village dwellers who over the eons had learned to see the universe as a womb for the soul's development. The heritage of that vision survived in America's first cities, which were built along lines dictated by the primordial shamanic mapping of the cosmos that these peoples rightly intuited as a legacy deserving fuller development. That something went wrong along the way is evident not only from the Mesoamerican equation of the rise of the city with the mythical fall of humanity out of a state of spiritual perfection, but from the actual course of historical events.

The notion that civilization is a necessary evil with as-yet-unforeseen consequences is a very old idea, but its usefulness in understanding the often disastrous course of human history is perhaps not yet exhausted. In Mesoamerica we find this idea expressed in myth and enacted in history to the point where separating the two becomes all but impossible. But whether it is depicted as myth or history or both, its central implication for humankind—that cultural productions entail a loss of focus on spiritual realities that must be guarded against at every turn of human development—remains the same and demands to be taken into account. The Mesoamerican civilizations were struggling to do just that, and in the record of that struggle lie the first outlines of a conception of the soul resilient enough to withstand the confusions of meaning that occur with each increase in human cultural complexity.

In line with this, it is possible to interpret the brutal rites of war and kingship as practiced throughout the high period of Mesoamerican culture as first fumblings at a new economy of the spirit: an economy based on the same warping and redefinition of the psyche that prehistory's shamanic teachers had intuited to be an essential experience in the lives of all men and women.

The details of this new economy are hinted at in Maya myth and ritual, in the tales of Quetzalcoatl Topiltzin, the man-god of the Toltecs, and in the bizarre details of the Aztec sacrificial drama. A nascent redefinition of the shamanic initiatory scenario is evident even in the games practiced in these cities, especially the well-known Mesoamerican ball game. The court on which this game was played from Olmec up to Aztec times appears to have functioned as a model, not of the universe itself as did the pyramid, but of one particular part of it: the subterranean amphitheater where souls were torn to pieces and remade by the tutelary demons that shamans had been describing for thousands of years before Maya artists took to depicting them in horrible detail on their stoneworks and funerary ceramics. Behind the evil appearance of these demons, as behind all the more onerous motifs of Middle American thought and culture, lay the promise of a fabulous kingdom of color and light—one for which the human soul is homesick whether it knows it or not but into the precincts of which it is only allowed after passing through a refining and finishing process of sometimes fearful dimensions. This was the paradise that the architects of pyramid and temple had sought to mirror on earth but which in the end they succeeded only in obstructing, thanks to a series of intertwined confusions and misplaced emphases that arose in the minds of those who built these structures up around themselves.

The record of other ancient civilizations has demonstrated that at a certain point in the unfolding of human consciousness and human culture it begins to be realized that this kingdom of light is a treasure of far greater worth than any of the many material approximations humankind is capable of creating of it, and that the spiritual treasure itself and its material symbols are at all costs not to be confused. In many ancient urban cultures, prevention of such a confusion between interior and exterior, spirit and flesh, was provided by mystical traditions that existed and functioned within the world of material power while remaining apart from it. In India, China, and elsewhere, the crazed building of ostentatious temples to the gods was tempered by the assertions of wandering monks and ascetics who through poverty and intense meditative introspection had learned to spot the dangers inherent in confusing the outer kingdoms of material wealth with the interior kingdoms of spiritual knowledge. Such figures led a centuries-long counterattack against the disorientating temptations of material power—an attack that the historical record demonstrates was sadly often less than successful. As the ordered, if humble, world of the primitive village community was replaced by gargantuan and often tyrannical metropolises, mystical communities re-

sponded by launching all-out retreats from the physical world—
including the natural landscape that for so long had held a
nonantagonistic place in the scenario of spiritual unfoldment.
Heaven was taken down from its place behind the sky, and the
glories of nature were condemned as illusory and meaningless.

Would the Mesoamericans' spiritual critiques of the drawbacks
of their own societies eventually have led to such a vehement denial of the physical realm, or would the native American legacy of
respect and love for nature have prevented such a complete turn-
around, leading instead to a more balanced appreciation of the
play of matter and spirit? We have no way of knowing, but it does
seem likely from the evidence left behind that a solution of some
kind to the self-imposed problems of civilization would eventually
have been arrived at. In essence this solution might have involved,
among other things, a general reformulation of the lore and practices revolving around the orienting cosmic axis, of which the pyramid was such an important example, and a revalorization of the
visionary landscape first discovered by the shaman that would
once again allow its energies to invade and inform the day-to-day
realities of human life in spite of the distortions and distractions
created by urban life.

Such a transformation of focus would have taken a long time to
come about, but from the power and coherency of the external
kingdoms of pyramid and temple these peoples have left behind,
there is no doubt that they possessed the energy and ability to find
and enter that other, invisible city of spirit whose structures were
already becoming overgrown even in the times when the Mesoamerican pyramids were in the process of construction.

2

The Star Beneath the Earth

▼▼▼

If you have not lived through something, it is not true.

Kabir

V ERY EARLY ON, at least fifteen hundred years before Christ and possibly much earlier, a presence began to take shape on the Gulf Coast of Middle America—a being compacted out of wind, waves, and falling waters, whose essence was movement and whose body was that of a snake. This snake lived in the sky and his presence there was everywhere apparent. Tornadoes got their invisible, horrific power from him. He was in the shapes that the clouds took, and in the texture of the winds that drove them across the sky. He was in the thick, meandering curtains of storm rain and the pulsing rivulets of water they left behind. Sometimes this serpentine genius of skies would even throw down tiny models of himself with the rains: baby snakes that slipped into clefts in the earth to rouse the souls of the things that slept there.

This sky snake had a counterpart that lived in the ground, and between the two of them they divided up the universe. Sleepy and cold, the second snake was very different from its brother in the sky. Its huge form vegetated in the black earth and stirred only to devour things. The stars entered its stomach when they dropped beneath the horizon, the spirits of corn and other crops were known to descend there when their stalks grew pale and withered, and humans, when their bodies were broken by war or accident or age, went there as well. The stomach of this snake was as long as the earth is wide, and a number of possibilities awaited the beings that traveled along its length.

Earth and sky had many names and many shapes in Mesoamerica. A single people might have five or six seemingly incompatible conceptions of what the plain of land and the dome of space above it were really most like. The sky might be described as a two-headed dragon, a giant snake, or a house of four iguanas. The earth, in addition to appearing as a four-cornered, wedding-cake-shaped "house" such as was mirrored by the pyramid, could also take on a number of quite different shapes and capacities. When people discussed questions of orientation and navigation, either of the road of life or of the levels of the spirit realm that awaited them at death, earth and sky most often appeared as houses; but when matters of war and sacrifice were discussed, the earth, especially its interior, might change into a giant amphitheater or ball court; likewise, when questions of the ultimate meaning of life arose, the universe might suddenly become a giant tree, with the earth's surface corresponding to the trunk and the roots forming a tangled map of the underworld.

But because both earth and sky were first and foremost seen as living entities, their shape and character were most often described, probably from the earliest times, in terms of an animal of one sort or another; the animal most often chosen to represent both regions was a snake. The same Olmecs who gave Mesoamerica its first pseudopyramid have left behind a series of stone reliefs depicting serpents that fly through the air and whose long bodies occasionally dissolve into a series of stylized volutes that probably were meant to symbolize rain-laden clouds. This mysterious civilization also laid down large, laboriously assembled mosaics in the earth beneath their cities—mosaics about which little is known today other than that they were probably designed to be permanently invisible to the people who made them, and that their shapes resemble, to some modern observers, the face and body of a giant snake.

Like the cultures that followed them, the Olmecs were an agriculturally sophisticated people. Maize was probably their staple crop, and it is guessed from some of their sculptures and rock carvings that they saw this grain and the plentiful snakes living in the fields where it grew as being very closely related. Snakes and corn do in fact share a number of similarities, ones that may seem strained to us but which were obvious enough in the days before science had arrived to classify and explain all of creation in its own more rigorous but sadly less whimsical terms. Corn kernels are shiny and regular, and are vaguely reminiscent of scales; the first green shoots of a corn stalk sprout from the ground in a "Y" shape that if caught at the right time looks surprisingly like a snake's forked tongue; also, both ears of corn and snakes share the ability of being able to slip easily out of their skins—a phenomenon that was still being remarked upon in Aztec times, when the shed skin of a serpent, the leaves enfolding a tufted ear of corn, and the skin of flayed sacrificial victims were treated as intertwined visual metaphors for the regenerative abilities of seasons, plants, and gods.

These similarities were more than mere curiosities to the peoples who first noticed and remarked upon them in their sculptures and myths. They were hints given by the universe to mortals, which if properly interpreted could tell them important things about the nature and destiny of their lives. Much energy and imagination went into their decipherment. The results of these investigations have much to teach us not only about the similarities between natural objects we might never have thought to compare, but more importantly about the similarities of the human imagination as it works among peoples distanced from each other by enormous geographic space.

Mircea Eliade often suggested in his writings that the men and women of modern societies are closer to their primitive neighbors than they would sometimes like to imagine.[1] One of his favorite examples of the misconceptions people use to maintain this distance is the notion that primitive peoples, in addition to being somewhat simpleminded in relation to the enlightened members of modern society, enjoy by virtue of this simplemindedness a happy freedom from those basic human problems that plague advanced civilization. Somewhere, it is thought, a place must exist where such plagues as fear, alienation, and cupidity have not yet reached, and the less clothing a people wears, the ruder the shelters in which they sleep, the more likely they are to be candidates for this position in the eyes of others. The rarity and possible nonexistence of any such people on earth had already been plentifully suggested a hundred years ago by such insightful expatriates from modern society as Herman Melville and Joseph Conrad. News that the Fall, whenever it occurred, left no villages or cities intact is given in their South Sea writings, and is present as well in the distant, preoccupied gazes of Gauguin's Tahitian women.

As Eliade points out, this common nostalgia for the naked integrity of paradise is a universal emotion, shared alike by people who wear many clothes and those who wear none at all. The memory of a precultural Eden, and the story of a fall from that first world into the present one ruled by the great trinity of work, sex, and death, has been recorded by many primitive communities in terms surprisingly similar to our own. The original world is often described in native American myth as one in which men and animals were brothers who spoke the same language and shared the same happy concerns. In these innocent times everybody lived forever and lacked for nothing, or at least thought so until someone—a man or a woman or an aberrant couple—developed a set of cravings for which this first environment did not provide, and through the pursuit of their satisfaction brought everything crashing down upon themselves.

Because of this initial break, the lives of humans, and sometimes even of plants, rocks, and animals, became pale and graceless imitations of what they had been before. But in spite of this falling away from perfection, the earmarks of that first exalted condition remained, in the form of subtle correspondences—such as, for example, the series of resemblances between snakes and corn—that if read correctly provided clues on how the joys of that first world might be recovered. If we are mistaken in envying primitive communities their supposed innocence, we perhaps would not be so wrong in admiring the strategies and hopes that some of those communities had for recovering it. These peoples at their most inspired saw the earth and the creatures upon it as fellows in a common longing and potential partners in a common project: the recovery of that first unbroken condition when the thoughts and desires of men and women were in fluid and absolute accord with the terrestrial and animal energies surrounding them.

The outlines of this unity were not easy to perceive or understand in the world as it was, however, nor were they without a terrible side. The gods of nature were larger, more numerous, and infinitely more powerful than mortals, and though those varied forces appeared to be calling men and women back into their company, it was not known what those forces would do with them once they had got them there. In Mesoamerica no animal—with the possible exception of the jaguar—came close to the snake in terms of its capacity to represent these ambiguities of the universe and its hidden intentions.[2] All things glorious and all things ghastly converged in its sinuous and hungry form, which over the course of Mesoamerican history was modified and improved upon in ways that made that duality even more apparent. At some point in the hazy stretch of centuries between the collapse of the coastal Olmecs and the rise of the Maya in the lands to the south and inland—some time around or before the year one in our calendar—the airborne version of the Olmec serpent began to be

represented in a sumptuous coat of feathers. This strange combination of elements created a religious symbol of incredible power:
whether as Gukumatz, Kukulkan, or Quetzalcoatl, as he was variously known to the peoples of Guatemala, Yucatan, and Mexico,
the feathered serpent became Mesoamerica's most oft-produced
image. It has proven attractive to outsiders as well, and has been
widely interpreted by writers in our own century. People have seen
in Quetzalcoatl a transparent metaphor for divinely sublimated
sexuality, a Mexican equivalent of the Chinese Yin-Yang, and
countless other things besides. Yet to those who first developed it,
the feathered serpent was probably most closely connected with a
group of ideas not about sexuality or cosmic unity per se, but
about an activity that in those times was believed to embrace these
concepts: ingestion.

The fate of most things in the natural world is to be eaten. This
fact was not lost upon the ancient Mesoamericans, who, because
of their ability to see not only plants and animals but the entire
body of earth and the planets wheeling above it as living and
thoughtful entities, imagined the process of ingestion going on in
places that we no longer consider. People, plants, planets, even the
span of day itself—the earth had only to hold still and eventually
all of these things, along with everything else on its surface and in
the sky above it, would pass into its depths. Some of these bodies,
like the sun, descended and returned frequently and regularly from
earth's interior. Others, like corn, descended less often but took a
much longer time to come back. Still others, like the planet Venus,
had complex and seemingly irregular schedules of descent and return, whose secret logic was known and discussed only by an elite
few.[3]

All of these entities and everything else besides descended into
the belly of the earth; yet only the individual and particular human
soul appeared to descend and stay.[4] It was this strange refusal on
earth's part to give back only this of all her varied foods that first
indicated to the Mesoamerican mind that there was something
distinctly different about the human position in the cosmos.

Snakes live in the earth and have the profoundly unsettling
habit of ingesting their victims alive. Even in the hard-headed
twentieth century, the sight of a snake's distended jaws closing
over its wide-awake and often warm-blooded prey seems almost
intentionally creepy. In ancient Mesoamerica, where the shapes

and habits of all the beings with which mortals shared the earth had something to say about the intentions of that world toward them, the effect of such a sight must have been infinitely more direct and powerful.

Yet because they were determined to engage the devouring world beneath them in a conversation that might give answers to the riddles of suffering and death, these early watchers of the earth and its creatures did not turn away from the serpent and its horrible habits but instead performed upon them the first in a series of mythic elevations that became something of a tradition in Mesoamerica, and of which the Aztecs became the undisputed masters. These elevations consisted in finding the worst, most repellent, and frightening phenomena possible and then focusing on them relentlessly in the intellectual explorations of myth and sculpture. By doing so, these thinkers ensured that their picture of the universe was an honest one, cognizant of all the cruel and frightening contradictions that life on earth entailed. As it happened, the devouring mouth of the snake proved to be a particularly potent locus of spiritual significance. Several hints from the pristine world of origins were found to be condensed there, and these hints became expanded and developed into a paradoxical set of assertions about the nature of the world around which the high civilizations that followed built their various but essentially related mythologies.

When it was first drawn up, probably at a time long before the rise of the Olmecs, this identification stated that while on her surface the earth often appeared to be a monster who devoured her children indiscriminately, beneath this facade she had a second, more profound side to her character.[5] This aspect cared for the human community and keenly wished to meet and speak with it, but it would do so only through the medium of an emissary capable of passing through her jaws and into the lands that existed beyond them.

Proof of this larger, more charitable landscape in the belly of the earth was provided not only by the daily and seasonal return of the stars, planets, and crops, which appeared to enter and exit from her belly unscathed, but more importantly by the experiences of those singular individuals blessed with the ability to die while still alive: the shamans around whose ecstatic trances the religious lives of Mesoamerica's first wandering and planting communities were most probably centered. By virtue of a long apprenticeship to the tutelary geniuses of the earth itself, these men and women were capable of leaving their corporeal bodies behind and moving with the stars, traveling to worlds beneath and above the earth and returning from them not only intact but in possession of fabulous powers and wisdom resulting from the experiences conferred upon them there.

Behind the scenes of the encompassing spectacle of nature in whose midst they lived, these emissaries between the human and superhuman worlds learned a number of things that served to mold their conceptions of the form and direction of life on the planet; but the most important of these lessons was that the earth desired human souls for positive reasons. Her capacity to devour could lead the human victim/initiate into a series of adventures lying beyond the barriers of physical extinction. The wisdom of this terrible but finally intelligent hunger was not just intuited by the shaman; it was experienced on a profoundly authentic psychological level. For those who entered its depths and reemerged, the ground beneath their feet became a living and fathomless reservoir of psychic force, across the uncanny depths of which the villages of humanity were scattered like leaves atop a still, black lake.

All across the American continent (and elsewhere in the ancient world) this devouring ground was given much the same Janus-faced character of terror and hidden benevolence, one that, viewed in a certain light, is not far from some modern conceptions of the subconscious. Freud's image of the conscious ego as but the external boundary of an invisible matrix of fluid psychic energies that feed and inform it unawares is in its way a replica of the model of human intelligence given by a shamanic ecstatic, with important differences: in the latter model the ground of these energies is not "blind" but keenly intelligent, and exists not within the chemicals and neurons of the brain but outside it, in the actual ground upon which these peoples walked. Current researchers have taken Freud's model out of its strictly empirical setting, and in the process have brought the modern conception of the psyche even closer to the shaman's. Some investigators of the mechanics of schizophrenia and related psychopathological disorders have become so impressed with the parallels between shamanic, initiatory madness and their more problematic, twentieth-century equivalents, that they have adopted images and terms from shamanic traditions in an effort to recover the psychologically broadening and deepening potentialities that these disorders conceal.

Leaving the structured regularities of day-to-day life behind, shamanic neophytes typically descend into a subterranean region that at first experience appears to be fraught solely with malevolent demons anxious to undo them. There they are overwhelmed by these demons and forced to suffer procedures that usually involve cutting, burning, or other violent actions. The heads of certain Asiatic initiates are placed on an anvil by these tutelary demons, who hammer at them until they take the shape they want. Other neophytes, as we mentioned above, are thrown into cauldrons and cooked for days. "Pieces" of their bodies—usually certain bones—are taken from them and replaced by replicas forged in the underworld.

These rough, concrete actions apparently disguise a profound psychological metamorphosis, in which the conscious portion of the personality is introduced to and invaded by formerly unconscious levels with an intelligence all their own. These levels break open the frame of the formerly circumscribed ego and allow it henceforth to participate in an expanded dimension of experience, which, in the days before it was regarded as a dead mass of inert matter, the earth itself was thought to be principally involved in. Having been taken into the bowels of the earth and ripped open there by forces that rummage with his "insides" and keep some of them down there in the other world after releasing him, the shamanic initiate is no longer a being set apart from the energies of the earth. From then on he has the rains and breezes of the universe rattling through him at all times, and its moods and energies are always partly his own.

These lessons of the vertiginous and potentially disorienting abyss upon which the house of human consciousness so precariously sits are as valuable today as they were thousands of years ago when they were first discovered. Now, however, the ones who usually gain an insight into that abyss are individuals perilously unequipped to deal with the forces they find there. Without a coherent and culturally ingrained tradition to receive their shattered psyches when they return to everyday reality, these modern "victims of the earth" risk living for the rest of their lives in a cold hell of fragmentation and nonmeaning out of which no path can be found.

Thanks to the work of a number of recent investigators of the unconscious wisdom at work in fear-generated psychoses, more and more of these unwitting initiates are learning how to use the fragmented intensity they encounter in the course of their psychotic breaks to construct a larger and more inclusive model of the reality they experience in their day-to-day lives.[6] Yet in spite of their successes, one crucial aspect of the psychic remending process is largely missing in these modern versions of the shamanic process: the earth and its role as receiver of the shaman's dreaming body. The most startling and liberating discovery that the shamanic initiate made in the course of these journeys was that the human identity is not bound to the physical body it is born into but is capable of moving out of it into realms existing beneath the earth and in the sky. It was on this newly experienced body that the demons of the underworld performed all of their operations, and it was this body that first felt itself to be taken into the mouth of the earth and chewed to bits.

Whether we call it the soul, the magical body, or any of a number of other names, this detachable entity underwent its adventures in realms that were never solely conceptual but which instead were connected with images of earth, fire, grasses, clouds, and animals. Without these grounding natural energies to receive it, the "out-of-body" experience, as it today is called, can become a somewhat sterile, indulgent venture, founded on a phantasmagoria of psychic imagery too dependent on the individual imagination and not enough on corresponding exterior forces. It was to greet and speak with those energies that shamans first left their bodies, and any model of psychic wholeness that pays tribute to those first adventurers must remember that their belief in the forces of nature as autonomous spiritual entities was a very serious one.

It may be that in the course of time those nonhuman energies at work in the earth and sky will be given a renewed status in the same way that Freud's subconscious was eventually broadened by his successors into a more subtle, intelligent, and less blindly impulsive entity. As it stands at the moment, even the most broad-minded researchers display timidity in this area, while those who take what are called the "earth spirits" seriously often display a less rigorous attitude toward them than did those shamanic adventurers who first risked a journey into their realm. Many now believe the living ground of earth to harbor energies that are alive in a more-than-simply chemical way, and if the earth ever does prove to harbor such a nonhuman consciousness, the shamanic and the psychological models of the universe might eventually show themselves to be even closer than we now imagine them to be.

Authentic shamans usually enjoyed a tremendous familiarity with the energies of this supporting but potentially engulfing supernatural ground, and when deprived of their attentions the entities inhabiting that ground might show their disapproval by becoming grumpy, sullen, or even lonely. Because so much of his "interior" or private self was connected to the surrounding world and the divine personages it contained, the shaman of necessity spent much time alone with these energies.

Speaking of shamanism among the Eskimo, Eliade says that many times a shamanic adept will take a dangerous ecstatic voyage—one that might leave his corporeal body prone and inert for more than an entire day—without a specific task in mind. "The Eskimo shaman," he says, "feels the need for these ecstatic journeys because it is above all during trance that he becomes truly himself; the mystical experience is necessary to him as a constituent of his true personality."[7] His adventures in the other world are manifold. Sometimes he has a spirit wife with whom he speaks or even copulates. But whatever the size and wonder of the things and personalities encountered in this realm, the shaman is able to bring only fragments back: like the hero of Hemingway's *The Old Man and the Sea*, he arrives in port only with the long white spine of the fish, as it were, and must work his whole life to do justice to the greater reality he encountered beyond the company of human beings.

The quirky reciprocity of shamanic interactions with the earth is illustrated by a well-known journey to the bottom of the sea taken regularly by some Eskimo shamans for the purpose of visiting Takanakapsaluk, the Mother of the Sea Beasts, a kind of submarine Earth Mother responsible for the well-being of humanity. In times of famine the shaman descends to a stone house at the bottom of the sea where Takanakapsaluk sits with matted hair by a fire, next to which the sea beasts themselves can be heard puffing and rolling in an enclosure. Eliade describes what follows:

> The goddess's hair hangs down over her face and she is dirty
> and slovenly; this is the effect of men's sins, which have almost

made her ill. The shaman must approach her, take her by the
shoulders, and comb her hair (for the goddess has no fingers
with which to comb herself).[8]

While he combs, the shaman explains to the goddess that there
are no seals in the upperworld, and the people are going hungry.
She gives the expected response that this is due to the people's
various sins and breaches of taboo. The shaman brings her response back to the citizens, who, assembled in his ecstatic house,
have been anxiously following his spirit's progress, guessing at its
location and activities through the twitches and murmurs coming
from his prone body. Returning to consciousness, he demands con-
fession from those who have transgressed the laws of the village.
These are forthcoming, and with their declaration the communal
guilt of the past months is done away with and the people begin
with a clean slate.

As is the case with so many shamanic interactions with the
divine world, this one tells more about the relationship of mortals
with gods through its incidental symbolism than through the de-
clared purpose of the visit. The shaman here, and the people he
represents, are more than servants or fodder to the submarine
mother who feeds them: they are her fingers. Without the human
extension of her force, the work of the world, that collaboration
between separate but intimately related energies, could not be
brought about, and the results would be disastrous.

The tenuous nature of that reciprocity was more apparent to the
shaman than anyone else, for he knew that he depended on the
benevolence of earth's entities for his very sanity. After the first,
shattering encounter with its energies, he no longer took any aspect of the splendidly ordered universe around him for granted.
Having experienced its destruction and remending through the lens
of his own, personally felt dismemberment, he was from then on
both united with it more strongly than others in his community,
and aware of the miraculous nature of those fluid, unseen struc-
turing energies by the grace of which the universe—and his
own identity which was now inseparable from that universe—
maintained their ordered complexity.

Twentieth-century psychiatrists have noted a similar, if less integrated manifestation of this gratitude in the labored geometric,
symmetrical constructions (usually drawings) sometimes produced
by patients recovering from psychotic episodes. These drawings

often take the same forms of centralized, quadripartite order as the shapes that primitive peoples inscribed on the bowls from which they ate, on their bodies, and which they also used as models for the shape of their cities.[9]

In the time of the Aztecs, those late and troubled inheritors of the Mesoamerican spiritual legacy, all intimacy with the forces of the universe had been lost, and the dynamic balance between cosmic order and psychological chaos, which the shaman once had tended, was slipping dangerously out of balance. Not only did their cities take on an aggressively relentless geometry; this unique people populated their over- and underworlds with demons whose outlines resemble the most inspired creations of modern-day psychotics. Their myths tell of a day when the vulnerable sun would be snatched from the sky and all order, value, and meaning would be shattered by hungry ghosts lurking just beneath the surface of a world whose seeming stability had all along been nothing but a cruel charade.

This disastrous transformation from an earth that constructively devours people to one that does so without gratitude or purpose took a long time to unfold, and its stages were recorded by the Mesoamerican cities that suffered it with impressive, if perhaps unintentional, accuracy. In addition to describing these changes in the earth's character as a gradual progression, the myths and images of the Maya and the Aztecs also treated that progression as being paralleled by a gradual loss of power and autonomy on the part of the individual human soul—a loss that was so devastating that its effects were mirrored in the vision these peoples had of everything in the natural world. In time, "mother earth" lost her first, ambivalent serpentine identity and took the form of other reptiles whose hunger was of a less ambiguous and more categorically evil nature. In the swamplands of the lowland Maya, earth became an alligator; while for the Aztecs it took a number of horrible forms, one of the most eloquent of which was the goddess Tlalteuctli, a monstrous toad whose entire body was alive with multiple, unblinking eyes and a series of mouths that croaked incessantly for human blood. When the earth turned against humanity the sky did so as well. The stars and planets that humans had first positively identified themselves with came in time to be seen as allies of these malevolent, metropolitan earth deities—all but the sun which, possibly because it was associated with light and consciousness and order, was treated as a victim vulnerable to the knives of fire and ice that swarmed in the belly of the earth.

In Aztec times the sun was perpetually threatened with death, for the realm of darkness and confusion into which he descended every evening was thought to harbor forces far more powerful than the principles of integration he stood for. It was in terms of the doomed sun that the underworld most often transformed itself into a ball court, on which the sun faced a rival team of enemies with skills superior to his. These enemies were usually represented by the stars and the planet Venus, who together defeated the sun and put him to death on a sacrificial table at the nadir of the universe. This vision of the stars was complemented by others, which framed their nature in a more personal but equally malevolent way. As the Mimixcoa, or "The Four Hundred Ancestors" (four hundred in Mesoamerica was another way of saying "countless"), they represented the souls of the ancestral dead, who though they once were mortals now looked down with scorn upon the world where before they had lived as husbands, wives, and friends. For this inspired and somewhat tormented people, death generally either annihilated the human soul or made it into a hollow-eyed zombie that returned to the world of the living only to terrorize and cause misery.

These powerful mythic conceptions of isolation and cosmic betrayal are not the sort that typically come to mind when people think of Indians, who as the benign ecologists of popular imagination were supposed to have nothing but love and respect for the land that supported them. The astonishing thing about the Aztecs is that they somehow managed to continue loving the earth even after they had transformed its interior into an ever-hungry conglomerate of demons waiting to devour them. While some would say that their incredibly negative picture of the earth was the work of devious political rulers striving to cow the populace with threats of divine punishment, the Aztecs were in fact a people possessed of such unusually noble (if often quirky and unsettling) character that threats of hell made little difference in regard to their behavior in life, which was ruled by an ideal of excellence for excellence' sake. Knowing that, with few exceptions, they would end up extinct or estranged from and hateful of the people they left behind, they did not fall sway to political manipulations designed to give them false hope.

The Maya and the Hero Twins

It is in myth that the thread connecting the tradition of those first, positive encounters with the devouring earth enacted by the shaman to the later, sacrificial traditions of the cities can most vividly be traced. The oldest story in the *Popol Vuh* concerns the adventures of a pair of brothers in the earth's interior, which, in the version that has come down to us, is described as a very evil and unpleasant place. The structure of this originally shamanic tale is essentially quite simple. The two heroes, Hunahpu and Xbalanque, descend into an underworld crowded with greedy and uncharitable demons to avenge a defeat suffered there by their father and uncle. The story passed through many hands before being set down in Latin characters in the highlands of sixteenth-century Guatemala, and over time its simple plot became encrusted with references to beliefs and customs from every stratum of Mesoamerican civilization. Characters and situations from the story have been identified on funerary ceramics from the Classic Maya cities, and it has been postulated that the story was at that time part of a much longer drama that described in greater detail the soul's progressive navigation of the underworld. Though no one is sure of the exact shape the story took in those times, the fragments that have survived tell more about Classic Maya conceptions of the supernatural realm than any other single source.

The story begins in the middle realm of earth, where the father and uncle of the hero twins, who for calendrical reasons are called One and Seven Hunahpu, are invited by the lords of the underworld to a game of tlachtli, the sacred ball game practiced in Mesoamerica from earliest Olmec times.[10] One and Seven Hunahpu accept the invitation and descend innocently into the underworld, unaware that the lords have invited them into their kingdom solely for the purpose of sacrifice. Once there the brothers are subjected to a series of mock initiatory tests and ordeals, all of which they fail, and they are sacrificed by the underworld lords even before they have a chance to play the game of ball for which they were originally invited. Their bodies are buried in the underworld soil, with the exception of One Hunahpu's severed head, which is placed in the branches of a calabash tree by the ball court as a symbol of the lords' triumph.[11]

Throughout the Americas, individual identity and spiritual force were thought to be concentrated in the head—hence the popularity of scalping among the Plains tribes, and the use of shrunken heads as kingly ornamentation among the Maya. Not surprisingly, the calabash tree bursts into bloom shortly after One Hunahpu's head has been placed in its branches, and the underworld lords, fearful of the still-remaining power in the head, forbid anyone to go near the tree. This taboo is broken by an underworld maiden named Blood Woman. Approaching the tree, she is addressed by the still animated head of One Hunahpu, who spits into the palm of her hand and thereby renders her pregnant. The bizarre method and circumstances of this impregnation alert the reader or listener to the fact that the offspring of Blood Woman are likely to be superhuman beings of some sort, for in the ancient Americas as elsewhere in the world, virgin births were always portentous events.

When Blood Woman's pregnancy is discovered and she proves cagey about the father's identity, insisting that she has "known the face" of no man, she is slated for sacrifice by the underworld lords, who throughout the tale exhibit an unquenchable lust for hearts, blood, and sacrificial proceedings in general, calling for them on the most meager grounds like a group of aging alcoholics proposing toasts at the Club. A quartet of owl-demons is entrusted with the job of sacrificing her and bringing back her heart to the lords as proof of their deed. But at the last moment compassion for Blood Woman prompts them to spare her and substitute an imitation "heart," made from the sap of a croton tree, for hers. While the underworld lords are crowing in satisfaction over this false heart, Blood Woman escapes into the middle world, where she is reluctantly taken in by the mother of One and Seven Hunahpu.

Hunahpu and Xbalanque are born to Blood Woman there in the middle world and raised in the house of their grandmother, where they engage in a series of exploits that establish them as individuals of singular talent. Discovering the ball game equipment of their deceased father and uncle, the twins commence to learn the game and predictably develop into great players. Their practices on the ball court set up a great racket and the underworld lords, hearing it, send up an invitation to come and compete with them, hoping thus to lure the twins to the same doom that their father and uncle had suffered.

The twins accept and set out for the underworld after first assuring their grandmother, who in the time since their birth has grown somewhat fond of them, that their fortunes there will not be the same as their father and uncle's. To keep her apprised of their progress, they leave with her two ears of corn, which they plant in the center of the house. "When the corn dries up," they tell her, "this will be a sign of our death: 'Perhaps they died,' you'll say, when it dries up. And when the sprouting comes: 'Perhaps they live,' you'll say, our dear grandmother."[12]

With this pair of vegetable homing devices serving as indicators of their fate, the brothers descend to the lands beneath the earth, where they prove to be cannier than their predecessors about the underworld lords' real intentions. Trap after trap is set for them: they are forced to endure cheating on the ball court and nightly imprisonment in a series of "houses" containing various demonic perils. Hunahpu (literally) loses his head one night when the two are imprisoned in a house of giant bats, yet through their magical abilities the twins are able to overcome this drawback, as well as all the other impossible tests put before them. At ease with the underworld's terrors from the start, they grow increasingly playful with their adversaries, eventually allowing themselves to be sacrificed in a giant oven, into which they gaily jump without any coaxing. Even this ordeal does not undo them: masters of wizardry, they know the secrets of surviving death by incineration, and return to life by having their bones ground to powder and tossed into a river.

In the waters the twins congeal into a pair of giant catfish, emerging after a time in human form.[13] Disguising themselves as itinerant magicians, they travel about the underworld performing astounding magical feats that eventually get them invited to the courts of the unwitting lords. There the twins give a performance that ends in an impressive demonstration of their mastery of death. They first sacrifice a dog and bring it back to life, and then perform the same trick on a reluctant Xibalban of low rank. As a finale, Xbalanque sacrifices his brother before the astonished lords: "One by one his legs, his arms were spread wide. His head came off, rolled far away outside. His heart, dug out, was smothered in a leaf, and all the Xibalbans went crazy at the sight."[14]

Hunahpu then bounces back as good as new and the lords, overcome with excitement, demand that the twins perform the trick on them. "Very well," the twins reply. "You ought to come back to life. After all, aren't you death?"[15]

The principal pair of underworld lords are then sacrificed, but the twins do not bring them back to life. The remaining lords are

6. Hunahpu prepares to decapitate his brother Xbalanque in the depths of Xibalba. Illustration from a Classic Maya vase currently on display at the Metropolitan Museum of Art.

struck with terror, and the twins, revealing their true identity, chastise them for their past behavior and tell them how they are to act from then on:

> All of you listen, you Xibalbans: because of this, your day and your descendants will not be great. Moreover, the gifts you receive will no longer be great, but reduced to scabrous nodules of sap. There will be no cleanly blotted blood for you, just griddles, just gourds, just brittle things broken to pieces. Further, you will only feed on creatures of the meadows and clearings.[16]

Having thus humbled the underworld and its denizens, the twins hasten to the calabash tree where the head of their father has decayed to such an extent that it is scarcely more than a skull. They attempt to engage the head in conversation, but having little success they instead deliver a speech in which they promise that, though he is gone from them, his name will be remembered and appropriately venerated. In other words, they comfort him through assurance that he will live on through his survivors. They then ascend out of the underworld into the dawn of the present age, either becoming or taking possession of the sun and the planet Venus. The action thus comes to a halt at an observable and very important astronomical event—the rising of the sun into the light of a new day with Venus moving just ahead of it.

Celestial descents and returns form the armature of many Mesoamerican myths, which in the course of their unfolding usually explain the motives and conflicting energies that surround the visual phenomenon. Venus, especially in terms of its relationship to the sun, was held to be the most important of these closely watched bodies, for in its manifestations both as morning and as evening star, its actions seemed to have a particularly vivid intentionality. In the evening, as the light drained out of the sky and flooded in a garish spread across the western horizon, the evening star rose into view just as the last of the sun's powers were giving out and it was preparing to endure its torturous journey across the underworld. Likewise, at dawn when the sun emerged for yet another pass across the sky, the morning star appeared for a known span of days and either led it up out of the depths or struggled to prevent it from emerging, depending on the myth in question.

The plots of myth and the patterns of the night sky were often very intricately aligned. In the above story, both the twins and their defeated uncle and father, One and Seven Hunahpu, "stand" for the sun and Venus, respectively in their rising, triumphant, morning manifestations, and their sinking, endangered, evening ones. Disguised celestial references appear throughout the story, and probably many more wait to be found. These celestial correspondences mesh with the story's many vegetable references to form a complex statement of the interwoven and finally very similar fates of plants and planets. Beneath this complex web of astronomical and agricultural references, however, there can still be seen a pair of essentially shamanic descents into the maw of the underworld; in the conflicting information that the story gives about these descents we can read the whole story of earth's gradual transformation from a potential friend at a slight remove from human beings to a monster hungry for their blood.

The landscape through which both pairs of brothers pass is entirely shamanic, its ball court geography retaining traces from the earlier times when it had been the belly of the initiatory beast. On their way to the underworld, the first pair of brothers pass through a narrow canyon and a river of clashing knives, which together are subtly suggestive of a *vagina dentata*, or toothed vagina. Women equipped with this unusual organ are a common motif in American Indian mythology, and it could also appear—as here—on a larger scale as a seductive but dangerous opening in the earth herself. Though one might be tempted to see this mythological organ as a cheap male jibe at womankind, it is actually a wonderfully concrete symbol for the ambiguous nature of the human condition itself. A vagina equipped with teeth suggests that the womb is not only a place of growth but a place of destruction as well—a hungry stomach that rips and rends all who enter it. To pass between the grinding maternal/sexual teeth into the bowels of the earth is to risk being devoured for the sake of ultimately being reborn.

Both sets of brothers, upon their arrival in the underworld, are forced to spend a night in a "house of darkness," the first in a series of testing enclosures that the first pair of brothers are not equal to but which Hunahpu and Xbalanque endure successfully. In the existing version of the story, these houses appear to be purely negative in character: the lords put each pair of brothers in them simply because they want to dispose of them as quickly as possible. But these underworld houses at some point possessed a more benign character. Along with the oven into which the twins finally leap, they are structures whose horrible contents (darkness,

animated knives, ferocious animals) originally served to remake
the persons who entered them instead of destroying them completely. As it turns out, Hunahpu and Xbalanque do indeed survive their stays in these enclosures, but the important twist to the
story is that they do so in spite of the underworld lords' wishes to
the contrary.

These underworld lords are the mouthpieces of the earth itself,
which speaks through them as an entity whose original, ferocious
charity has degenerated into a wild lust for the spectacle of extinction. Having entirely lost their hidden, tutelary dimension,
these demons are no more than cheaters and pompous fakes,
wholly unworthy of veneration, as a verse toward the end of the
tale makes clear:

> Their ancient day was not a great one,
> these ancient peoples only wanted conflict,
> their ancient names are not really divine,
> but fearful is the ancient evil of their faces.[17]

These "masters of stupidity, masters of perplexity" possess the
same qualities of excessive pride, hatred of the living, and lust for
the spectacle of blood that characterized the stellar and underworld demons of the Aztecs—demons who, despite the brothers'
hopeful pronouncements to the contrary, continued to receive
oceans of sacrificial blood from the metropolitan cities right up to
the time of the Conquest. Yet the landscapes in which these demons sit were at one time populated by other personalities of
which they are but a residue: a chorus of otherworldly voices that
at first had been separated from humanity only by a modest barrier, whose perimeters they stepped over with ease and frequency.
As human culture advanced, this barrier became a wall with fewer
and smaller openings, and those beings were left alone to grow
ugly from neglect.[18]

These purely malicious beings are the disinherited relations of
the demons of the pure shamanic mode, whose threatening appearance had always masked an ultimately beneficial purpose. A
good example of the latter is the Siberian Bird-of-Prey-Mother, a
demon described by Eliade as resembling "a great bird with an
iron beak, hooked claws, and a long tail. This mythical bird,"
Eliade continues,

shows itself only twice: at the shaman's spiritual birth, and at his death. It takes his soul, carries it to the underworld, and leaves it to ripen on a branch of a pitch pine. When the soul has reached maturity the bird carries it back to earth, cuts the candidate's body into bits, and distributes them among the evil spirits of disease and death. Each spirit devours the part of the body that is his share; this gives the future shaman power to cure the corresponding diseases.[19]

Keeping in mind the potentially positive meanings hidden in the story, we can now include some of its planetary aspects in our reading, for originally there was probably no hard conceptual separation between the rising sun and the shamanic dreamer returning to consciousness after the numbing initiatory journey. Whichever activity assumed the pattern first (a question that has something of the-chicken-and-the-egg about it, for human beings have probably been victims to ecstatic transports of one kind or another for as long as the sun has dawned upon their habitations), the descents and returns of the surrounding world had become so intertwined that their stories were all in essence the same. In its first, beneficent form, using the symbolism of the Maya and Aztec cities in the ways for which they had originally been intended, the plot of this drama was essentially psychological, and the shared movements of the universe were but paraphrases of it. It went something like this:

Like a bug-eyed mouse disappearing down the gullet of a perennially smiling serpent, the mumbling initiate sinks into madness. His soul, like a fallen sun, wanders across a plain of darkness, catatonia, and vegetable silence. Invisible enemies crowd around. His bearings robbed from him, he soon loses all sense of direction and must be led to the circular stone at the nadir of the world, where the red coal of his consciousness will be broken into a thousand shards. The sharpened stone comes down, and he flies off in all directions, broken wide. It is then, at this point of total extinction, that a reversal comes. After all has been destroyed, something still remains. One by one his senses return, the senses he had thought were the whole of his identity but which were in fact only the dressings of an unfathomable core: a still-breathing center around which the returning fragments of his personality now arrange themselves. Having suffered through the catastrophic attack, he now feels lighter than air. Black claustrophobia and confusion have given way to a sense of triumphant buoyancy. Floating at ease in the transparent world, he watches the sharp-faced demons retreat, their work done. In his stiff joints he feels the jewels of eternity they have hammered into him.

Like Alice after she has drunk her cup of tea, like the morning sun burning off the mists and shadows of the once again visible land, the recovering victim feels himself breaking through the roof of the circumscribed world and his gaze penetrating to the ends of the four directions. Here is a description of an Eskimo initiate's experience of such a restructuring aftermath:

> It is as if the house in which he is suddenly rises; he sees far ahead of him, through mountains, exactly as if the earth were one great plain, and his eyes could reach to the end of the earth. Nothing is hidden from him any longer; not only can he see things far, far away, but he can also discover souls, stolen souls, which are either kept concealed in far, strange lands or have been taken up or down to the land of the dead.[20]

This lucid and all-encompassing vision is very similar to that enjoyed by the first four humans of the *Popol Vuh* as described in the first moments after they have come to life:

> Thoughts came into existence and they gazed; their vision came all at once. Perfectly they saw, perfectly they knew everything under the sky, whenever they looked. The moment they turned around and looked around in the sky, on the earth, everything was seen by them without any obstruction. . . . As they looked, their knowledge became intense. Their sight passed through trees, through rocks, through lakes, through seas, through mountains, through plains.[21]

Whenever it occurs in the shamanic tradition, this original clarity of vision is related to a living earth that, like the individual human, has partially fallen away from its original, primordial lucidity and brilliance and which seeks the partnership of humans to once again regain these vanished qualities. Such a recovery necessitates a collaboration between humans and the homesick energies of nature that is dangerous but ultimately worth whatever perils are entailed. The power that this call for a collaborative reawakening holds for the human imagination did not entirely fall away with the shamanic cultures which first gave voice to it, but can show up in the modern consciousness as well, as it does in the poem "The Half-Finished Heaven" by the Swedish poet Tomas

Tranströmer. This poem speaks in tones of an earth-conferred clarity reminiscent of shamanic narratives and starts with a hint of the corresponding period of paralysis and onslaught that preceded it:

> Despondency breaks off its course.
> Anguish breaks off its course.
> The vulture breaks off its flight.
>
> The eager light streams out,
> even the ghosts take a drink.
>
> And our paintings see daylight,
> our red beasts of the ice-age studios.
>
> Everything begins to look around.
> We walk in the sun in hundreds.
>
> Each man is a half-open door
> leading to a room for everyone.
>
> The endless ground under us.
>
> The water is shining among the trees.
>
> The lake is a window into the earth.[22]

Part of the power of this and other of Tranströmer's poems seems to lie in their refusal to leave the natural landscape out of the process of psychic integration. Aside from its intriguing references to the sudden transparency of that landscape, what makes this poem interesting in terms of the shamanic scenario and its echoes in the *Popol Vuh* is the mystery generated by the collaborative other—the suggestive "we" it uses. As the poet's vision spreads and rises out of the abyss of blindness and paralysis, a still-distant crowd emerges and moves with him into the open air—a crowd whose mystery is probably better left intact except to say that they have something to do with the dead, with the faces that appear in dreams, with the devils whose attacks had first made possible this release into freedom, and perhaps most importantly with the earth itself.

As the psyche's devourer and its partner in transformation, the spirit of the earth can become one or many, but what is essential is that the natural landscape be experienced as a partner, a witness, an entity that watches us and waits for the moment when it can join us in a movement toward a new condition of clarity and insight. This clarity is the liberating, essential, yet ultimately dangerous condition of the visionary, who in seeking to develop a dialogue with it must risk a plunge into the darker regions of the earth, where lies the very real potential of disorientation, madness, and blank extinction. When first the individual opens the amorphous contents of the soul to the chill winds of the transhuman realm, there is a chance that their invading currents will sweep his or her identity away into its larger energies. And yet if the lost landscape and its crowd of allies are to be recovered—if one's psyche is to become whole like it was in the time of the earth's first beings who saw everything and everywhere—this opening must be risked.

That lost collaborative spark, which resides in, and speaks for, the subterranean energies of earth, has taken many faces in the course of history: In the Orphic tradition it became a woman, a dead and departed lover beckoning silently from the enfolding shades, demanding of the descending dreamer an impossible feat of rescue. Pre-Columbian America was full of such myths, in which a man, usually the husband of a recently deceased spouse, risked a hazardous descent and various torments of an initiatory sort to recover his departed wife—a task that Eliade suggests connects this mythic tradition with the shaman's most frequent duty in the other world of rescuing a lost soul.[23]

In the version of the twins' descent that has come down to us, the climax of all the mock initiatory actions is their meeting with the spirit of their father as it languishes in the tree where the underworld lords had placed it. Given all of their other magical abilities, one would imagine that these accomplished magicians might have more than mere words of condolence for the father they have braved the terrors of the underworld to see, but such is not the case. By the time they get to the head of their father, it still functions as a last, enfeebled house for his soul, but it has decayed to such an extent that its face, the visible evidence of his identity as a unique being, is almost unrecognizable. A strange passage then relates how the twins attempt to have their father speak the name of each part of his body, for to do so would automatically bring those parts back. The head tries to do so but is able to name only his mouth, nose, and eyes: the names for the rest of the parts of his body escape him, which means that through forgetfulness, resurrection is denied him.

It is too late for the twins to do anything but deliver words of comfort. "You will be prayed to," they promise the head of their father. "Your name will not be lost. We merely cleared the road of your death, your loss, the pain, the suffering that were inflicted upon you." These words echo those that the head of One Hunahpu had spoken earlier to Blood Woman when he had impregnated her with his spittle—words that show that even then he was resigned to fading on the branches of the underworld tree instead of growing into a spirit of divine capacities.

> It is just a sign I have given you, my saliva, my spittle. This, my head, has nothing on it—just bone, nothing of meat. It's just the same with the head of a great lord: it's just the flesh that makes his face look good. And when he dies, people get frightened by his bones. After that, his son is like his saliva, his spittle, in his being, whether it be the son of a lord or the son of a craftsman. . . . The father does not disappear, but goes on being fulfilled. Neither dimmed nor destroyed is the face of a lord. . . . Rather, he will leave his daughters and sons.[24]

In numerous myths about the time of origins and the circumstances that led to humankind's present, momentarily reduced status as creatures whose spiritual abilities have been partially occluded, this falling away is attributed to and explained by a parental figure who through the act of giving birth inadvertently sets rolling the process of generation. After this first exemplary act of procreation, sex, birth, and death weave their troublesome matrix over that previous condition where everyone had lived in eternal and androgynous perfection. The words delivered here by One Hunahpu might originally have taken the form of such a parental speech, delivered apologetically to the world's first conventional offspring by the parent whose slipup had brought death into being. But if, in that original version, One Hunahpu had died after delivering his talk, it most likely would have been with the promise of returning at a point far in the future when the period of divine occultation came to an end. This is the promise often contained in the American Orpheus myths as well: if the departed spouse must stay in the Beyond, she does so with the implication of a day to come when husband and wife (and by implication the worlds of mortals and of the spirits of nature) will once again converge to form that lost, apocalyptic unity for which both sides yearn.

In this version that promise has been lost. Originally intended to place the shortcomings of the human condition in a larger context, it instead now betrays the loss of that promise through the death of the immortal, dreaming body, the soul-essence through whose workings the worlds of mortal humans and of the immortal gods and spirits had before remained at least in partial contact. This was the detachable, shamanic soul, capable of surviving the body's disintegration, whose playful and elastic nature the twins had demonstrated so vividly when they grabbed each other by the arms and jumped willingly into the oven the lords had prepared for them. Occurring as the climax of the catalog of their feats, the twins' agreement with the fading face of their father that they can do nothing to save him and that he will never, ever be seen or heard from again signals the death of the living shamanic tradition and the birth of a new species of immortality: an ersatz and pale version known as lineage.

In the later years of the great Maya cities, it is likely that the gaudy spectacle of kingship, while retaining the shamanic symbolism of survival of the underworld's terrors and rebirth in the stars, was gradually brought to focus entirely on blood lineage. As the secrets of the living earth were forgotten or atrophied into sterile doctrines passed on only by priestly elites, the disembodied soul, the dream body experienced concretely by the shaman, became more and more a topic for debate and less a living reality. The head of One Hunahpu speaks for all kings both in his forgetfulness of the lost promise of a "body" suited to the ovens and iceboxes of the underworld and in his pretense of satisfaction with living on through his sons. It was that acceptance that made the underworld ovens deadly instead of transformatory, and it was that forgetfulness that had given the demons who ran them an eternal and malicious hunger instead of a desire to be revealed as disguised teachers of the soul.

It is but a short step from the loss of authentic spiritual powers to obsession with material ones. Having chosen through their forgetfulness of authentic spiritual practice and experience to read the ciphers of the natural world as messages of individual doom, the Maya stonecutters devoted the hieroglyphics that crowd the borders of their reliefs to information primarily concerned with who descended from whom, who captured whom, and from whom the captive him- or herself descended. As the martial strength of these cities continued to grow, the saving forces of the supernatural landscape shrank in proportion.

For the shaman, the sky is, as the Bakairi people of South America say, "no higher than a house."[25] But in Mesoamerica, at least, it appears that as the shaman's abilities atrophied, the sky retreated further and further, entailing ever larger ritual platforms built atop ever larger pyramids to reach it. The walls separating the human from the supernatural worlds became rock-solid, and instead of descending into the few remaining gaps in those walls, which required ever greater concentrations of physical violence to produce, the urban rulers threw in victims with messages of goodwill attached—victims that never returned with news of how the messages were taken. Rescue gave way to revenge and torture—the mundane kind we know today. These took the place of that ultimately beneficial harrowing that had been worked upon the magical body beyond the perimeters of the human sphere, in that larger and now tragically alienated landscape without which the project of Mesoamerican civilization became an ordeal without purpose, a quest without a treasure.

It was, then, not so much a fall from innocence that these cities were suffering from, as from the loss of a larger form of experience. Despite their frenzied attempts to take solace in the false eternity provided by the cult of lineage, the specter of the soul's extinction and the corresponding meaninglessness of all human life loomed so large upon these cities that the movements of the planets—which before had been read as messages of human possibility—were reinterpreted as a set of recurring murders that paralleled those occurring on the sacrificial blocks of the cities. The Aztecs went so far as to advance the idea that the sun of each new morning was an entirely different entity from the one that had made its exit into the realm of darkness and uncertainty the night before. In other words, the disastrous plot of the *Popol Vuh* repeated itself every night for them—a plot in which no one is rescued, no reconciliations between mortals and the spirits of earth occur, and all the fires and dismemberments serve not to change or renew the soul but instead annihilate it forever.

As the lid of the tomb of Pacal in the Temple of the Inscriptions makes clear, the peoples of the Classic Maya cities who were engaged in all this warfare were still at least theoretically interested in winning access to the celestial realm of immortality as stars in the night sky. Membership among that crowd was still won by surviving the tests of the underworld, but it appears that in the course of Maya history that celestial region became harder and harder to enter—perhaps because its actual existence as a haven for the human soul was increasingly doubted. Though Pacal and his fellow kings were probably instructed by the priestly elites to follow a course of action similar to the one taken by Hunahpu and Xbalanque through the successive annihilatory "houses" of the underworld, these kings most likely were starting to suspect that their chances of surviving those houses were as slim as the rest of the population's. The intentions of the earth were changing, and more and more it came to be believed that whatever a person's status in the human world, once he or she was taken into the belly of the earth, the forces at work there would, in the words of the *Popol Vuh*, "hide their face" forever.

By Aztec times, the underworld was not even theoretically a path to the stars—which in any case had by then become a charmless wasteland populated by airborne ghouls—but an end in itself. Good and evil alike descended there, to wander for a span of exactly four years before reaching that block at the world's nadir where their soul-essence was annihilated completely. The earth was no longer a living reservoir of collaborative spiritual energies but an ever hungry reptile whose many mouths led nowhere. The realm of initiation had become a crypt.

The Aztecs and Quetzalcoatl

The Aztecs were very likely the most death-obsessed civilization that the world has ever produced, but this does not mean, as has often been suggested, that their brief reign was nothing more than a melancholy capstone to the greater achievements of those who came before them. Far from inventing warfare and ritual sacrifice, the Aztecs inherited them along with the rest of a problematic cultural tradition that for a thousand years had depended on those practices to give order and meaning to human life. Much more is known about Aztec sacrificial practice—its methods, meanings, and cost in terms of human well-being—than about the act as it was undertaken by more ancient peoples like the Maya. But from the evidence available it appears that most of its essential elements had been in use for centuries before the Aztecs fastened upon it as the greatest and most mysterious of all human activities. Picking up where those before them had left off, the Aztecs refined the arts of warfare and sacrificial death and reinterpreted the mythological worldview connected with them, showing in the course of this reinterpretation how it was that these practices had come to be at once the most essential and the most unbearable aspect of life in the Mesoamerican city.

Because their grasp of the civilizations that came before them was incomplete, and because they spent so much of their time engaging in sacrificial displays of a drama and intensity unmatched by any other ancient people, the Aztecs are often treated as callous vulgarians who merely aped the subtleties of the older Mesoamerican religions without understanding anything of their esoteric meanings. In fact, the Aztecs might have been, in their eccentric way, not only one of the most insightful of all Mesoamerican peoples, but one of the most earnestly religious as well. The combination of morbidity and aesthetic sensitivity that made up the Aztec character shows, if examined with compassion and open-mindedness, that something much more significant than the exigencies of political power or simple force of habit had kept the sacrificial tradition alive in Mesoamerica for so many centuries. Despite its enormous flaws, the sacrificial drama retained within it the earmarks of the shamanic initiatory tradition, and had functioned over those centuries as a provisional doorway into regions of human experience of tremendous power and subtlety; the Aztecs came closer than any of their predecessors to achieving the practice's potential as a misguided but nevertheless effective method of achieving contact with the gods.

The Aztecs put a great deal of effort into streamlining the sacrificial process so that it was capable of accommodating the maximum number of victims a metropolitan city could provide. So efficient did their priests and politicians become at this that the death tolls in the Aztec cities at their height reached proportions unheard of on the continent before their rise to power. It is the sheer volume of victims that this process claimed that, more than anything else, makes the Aztecs so difficult to approach with understanding or compassion. Yet behind these statistics there is evidence that the killers were as much victims of the sacrificial act as those they killed, for they were involved in a misdirected but profoundly felt spiritual adventure whose end goal was reattainment to the lost world of spirit that had retreated so disastrously with the rise of the Mesoamerican cities. Whereas the Maya appear to have practiced human sacrifice primarily as a method of personal, individual aggrandizement, sacrifice among the Aztecs was a far greater entity than the priests and political functionaries who performed it. The Aztecs' desire to come to terms with their destructive compulsions emerges piecemeal in their recorded myths and speculations, and their astoundingly violent way of life becomes comprehensible only when one sees that violence as a means of addressing a universe governed by forces that had come to be seen as equally harsh and unforgiving.

Sacrifice was a primary cosmic principle in this universe—an a priori factor as important as time and space, and hence an essential tool for human beings desiring to enter into contact with the supernatural forces that gave shape to the world. Like those who came before them, the Aztecs justified sacrifice mythologically by asserting that the gods demanded human life and human blood for sustenance. (This was especially true of the sun, whose need for sacrificial blood in order to keep moving across the sky is the best known of all the Aztec rationalizations of the sacrificial act.) But behind their pantheon of ravenous gods lay a distinctly human frustration with the nature of creation and the seeming incompleteness of the human condition, which was in fact the deepest psychological impetus for the act's continuance. This same essential frustration shows up throughout human history, and over the course of time an enormous catalog of responses has been devised to cope with it. The Aztecs' particular set of responses was only partially realized and bizarre in the extreme, but the sincerity with which they struggled to formulate them out of the conceptual materials they had at hand cannot but incite admiration.

The Aztecs lived in a world increasingly deprived of those absolutes through which human consciousness seeks to anchor and orient itself. Those provided in former times by the shamanic tradition had degenerated and were in desperate need of reformulation—a reformulation that so far had not arrived. At bay in a malevolent and increasingly incomprehensible universe, the Aztecs observed that the single most irreducible fact of human life was mortality and fastened onto this insight with a vengeance, using the intentional staging of human death to punctuate and lend a sense of ultimate meaning to everything they did and stood for. Meanwhile, the contradiction inherent in sacrifice—that human life can be made "real" only by violent human death—gave rise to a confused and uniquely tormented understanding of the purpose and meaning of that life. Alternately enchanted and repulsed by the paradoxical nature of human existence and the ritual act that defined it, the Aztec cities saturated themselves in spec-

7. *Four characteristically death-oriented images from the* Codex Laud.

tacles of violence in order that, through constant repetition, the hidden mechanics they intuited to be lurking within them might come into sharper focus.

Sacrificial victims usually met their end abruptly in the Aztec cities. While the Maya appear to have indulged in gruesome and protracted tortures of their captives, the Aztecs were interested primarily in the instant of death and in the mental attitude that captive and killer adopted in the charged moments leading up to that instant. The break in ontological conditions undergone by a person passing from life into death—the all but seamless shift in cosmic states that occurs when a living, breathing, thinking individual becomes an inert body—was replayed constantly in the Aztec cities.

Victims would line up on the innumerable Aztec festival days before the steps of one of the many pyramids that anchored the Aztec cities with full knowledge of what awaited them on its summit, the queue sometimes stretching, it has been said, for lengths of a mile or more into the city's streets and avenues. Following one after another up steps that were black and slippery with the blood of those who had gone before them, each of these victims, upon reaching the temple at the summit, was seized and spread across a large, round, and slightly convex stone.[26] The victim's chest was swiftly broken open by a head priest with a heavy flint knife.[27] This same priest then reached into the victim's body and with his hands ripped out the still beating heart, which he held aloft for the approval of the four directions and the sun. The rest of the body, essentially as insignificant now as the sections that a rocket drops behind as it ascends into the heavens, was toppled forcibly back down the steps, in full view of the next ascending sacrificial candidate, who had to take care to dodge it as it tumbled past. When at last it came to rest at the base of the pyramid, the shattered, mannequinlike remnant of the body was decapitated, flayed, and hacked to pieces. The head of the now fully initiated member of the Aztec cult of death was placed upon one of the crowded tzompantlis, or skull-racks, that rose like billboards here and there in the Aztec cities, while the flayed skin might later be worn by a priest who fitted himself into the grisly garment like a diver squeezing himself into a rubber wet suit. The flesh itself was destined for consumption by the relatives and friends of the victim's captor, usually in a kind of stew composed of succotash and various other more conventional ingredients, at the cannibal feast that followed such ceremonies.

These horrific yet minutely choreographed parades from being into nonbeing were witnessed by the general public as well as the priestly and warrior elites, and gave daily life in the Aztec cities a surreal and nightmarish flavor that left its mark on every member of society. While it is beyond question that these profoundly unpleasant rites produced a psychic charge with important spiritual implications for the priests who performed them, they were also deeply damaging to the morale of the general populace. The constant demand for sacrificial victims that the priests' fascination with the event entailed put strains upon that populace that it could not have borne forever.

Of the volumes of Aztec myth and speculation taken down by clerics in the years following the Conquest, many are concerned, directly or indirectly, with the all-embracing ideology of sacrifice and the problems it created. Present throughout these writings, as a man, an anthropomorphized god, or in the sky-encompassing, serpentine form in which he had begun his term of rule in Mesoamerica, was the feathered avatar of the ancient Olmec sky-serpent, whom the Aztecs knew as Quetzalcoatl.

"Quetzalcoatl" literally means "plumed serpent," and while the Aztecs often envisioned the god as such and were responsible for many of the dramatic images that have made this beast so popular among twentieth-century artists and writers, this was only the first in a series of associations that the word conjured up for them. There is virtually no aspect of the Aztec universe that was not touched on in one way or another by this inexplicably popular god in one of his many guises. In addition to embodying the sinuous energies of clouds, rains, and winds, Quetzalcoatl could stand for the serpentine body of the underworld, while at the same time giving his name to the planetary and mythological personages who traveled along its length. Because the feathered serpent is the most plentiful and the most widespread of all Mesoamerican religious images, scholars have spent much time attempting to trace the course of its development, trying to understand along the way how it was that a dragon representing the elemental forces of winds and clouds would come to be the central religious figure of a civilization such as that of the Aztecs, dedicated as it was to the arts of war and sacrificial death. No completely satisfactory explanation has been found, but it appears that as his image was carried out of the Gulf Coast area where it was born and into the Yucatan, Guatemala, and central Mexico, Quetzalcoatl broke up into a number of different yet related gods, some of which take a human form, and which often appear to share nothing in common with one another except their name.[28]

Quetzalcoatl's capacities are so many and so varied that as a whole he would appear to have no definable character whatsoever. But if a single, broad association were to be chosen to define the god a case could be made that all of these disparate avatars are involved, in one way or another, with the journey out of human life that had first been practiced by the shaman and which ended up being practiced in such an unfortunately one-way fashion by the sacrificial initiate. The entire range of possibilities, the various potential boons and catastrophes that arise when a living body leaves the land of everyday experience and journeys to the realms of mystery that stretch beneath the earth and above it, took so many forms in Mesoamerica that—possibly—a single name and a single image were needed to tentatively unite those situations, in order that someday a concordance between all of them might emerge. That concordance was still being searched for in the time of the Aztecs, and because sacrifice was their principal tool for exploring the dimensions of meaning beyond the human sphere, they gave the name of Quetzalcoatl to many of the characters in their history and mythology who were involved with the problems of that particular method of exploration.

Feathered serpents are plentifully illustrated in Classic Maya stonework, but the meanings and associations this creature held for them are particularly foggy. Quetzalcoatl first appears in the *Popol Vuh* as Gukumatz, a glittering celestial serpent of the primordial waters who collaborates with several other creator gods in bringing forth the earth and populating it with humans. There is even speculation that one of the Hero Twins is in fact yet another avatar of Quetzalcoatl in disguise. In Aztec rewritings of the creation story, the gods increasingly desire mortals not because they need someone to talk to but because they want something good to eat. Here Quetzalcoatl takes the form a culture-hero, who is put in charge of recovering the bones of humans, left over from previous creations, from where they lie scattered in Mictlan, the Aztec equivalent of Xibalba. Like those of the Hero Twins at the climax of their underworld adventure, these bones contain the spirit-essence of humanity, which Quetzalcoatl and the other gods reactivate by crushing them into a powder that they mix with blood drawn from their penises. From this mixture emerge the Aztecs—in debt to the gods from the start and slated to spend the rest of their time on earth repaying it.

Quetzalcoatl is one of the few gods envisioned by the Aztecs as being, in some of his incarnations, at least mildly charitable toward human beings, yet these incarnations of the god are never more than partially successful in the favors they perform. Having wrested the bones of humans from the clutches of the lord of Mictlan, who like his Maya counterparts is a greedy and unpleasant individual unwilling to give up the life-essence of humanity once he has hold of it, the Quetzalcoatl of this myth suffers a momentary loss of consciousness while in the depths of Mictlan.

When he awakes, he finds that the bones that will give rise to the new generation of humans have been nibbled at by demons disguised as underworld partridges. The people created from these half-eaten bones turn out to be imperfect, subject to disease and various other shortcomings. Likewise, when he is sent in search of corn to feed these new charges he succeeds in finding it but not in bringing it all the way out of Food Mountain, in which the jealous gods of rain have stored it. As a result of his failure, humanity is forced to work for a living instead of getting its nourishment out of the earth for free. This flawed aspect continued to haunt Quetzalcoatl when he took the form of a mortal, as the Aztecs believed him to have done in the partly mythical city of Tula.

The historical Tula was a capital of the Toltecs, a late civilization that had risen from the ruins of Teotihuacan around A.D. 700. Unlike the civilizations that had preceded them, the Toltecs lasted only a few hundred years before the strains of metropolitan life drove them into collapse. The first Aztecs probably passed the ruins of this once great city around A.D. 1100, when they entered the valley of Mexico as part of a wave of hunting peoples descending out of the north in response to the new lands opened up by the Toltec collapse. These primitive peoples came into contact with the remaining vestiges of Toltec society and rapidly assimilated their agricultural lifestyle and the rudiments of the complex mythology that accompanied it. Not much is known about how these northern hunters lived before they encountered the vestiges of Toltec civilization, but it appears that as soon as they were given a taste of the benefits to be gained from an urban/agricultural lifestyle, they took to rebuilding what was left of Toltec culture with a vengeance. In less than two centuries the broken remnants of the Toltec world were reassembled in a new collection of city-states that together commanded almost all of Mexico. Driven by a mysteriously insatiable desire to conquer and subjugate, the Aztecs produced the most powerful empire that the American continent had yet known—an empire whose sole raison d'etre was warfare and sacrifice.

Lacking the insights of modern archaeology, these extraordinarily enthusiastic newcomers pieced together the history of the land they had taken over from what the remaining enclaves of Toltecs could tell them. The Toltecs had inherited much of their worldview from the Teotihuacanos, who had developed theirs in collaboration with the Maya peoples far to the south. These two cultures, it will be remembered, in turn owed many of their pivotal concepts to the Olmecs and the lesser Gulf Coast civilizations that came after them. This complex and centuries-long interplay of motifs and traditions was telescoped by the Aztecs into a single grand inheritance that they attributed entirely to the Toltecs. In their reworking of the Mesoamerican cultural legacy, the Aztecs credited their immediate predecessors with everything of value ever produced by humankind. Stonemasonry, architecture, weaving, astronomy, and divination—these skills and others were thought by the Aztecs to have been invented by the Toltecs, and pursued by them with consummate skill. The Tula of Aztec imagination was the city of cities: a center in such perfect alignment with the four corners of the universe that cotton sprung in colors from the fields around it and corn grew in such quantities that it was used as firewood.

In the midst of such splendor something was, of course, destined to go wrong. It is in the Aztec myths describing the fall of Tula and the beleaguered priest-king named Quetzalcoatl Topiltzin (Nahuatl for "Our Revered Prince") who rose and fell with it, that one finds the last and perhaps the greatest commentary on the ill-fated nature of civilization in Mesoamerica. Though it bears numerous general similarities to the huge body of native American myths that seek to explain the various inherent shortcomings of the human condition, this series of myths and legends is characterized by a distinctly urban focus on the sacrificial act as both the source of many of humanity's problems and the possible key to their resolution. In these myths, as in historical reality, urban growth and sacrificial practice went hand in hand: sacrifice is posited in them as the source both of Tula's rise and of its decline, and there occur here for the first time hints of a path beyond those practices—a path that gives the ubiquitous term "Quetzalcoatl" the most portentous association it was yet to receive.

To understand why the fall of Tula was so important an event for them, we must first give a clearer picture of the world in which the Aztecs lived—particularly those aspects of Aztec life that pertained directly to warfare. Tenochtitlan, the capital of the Mexica Aztecs, was constructed in a very short time and flourished for only about a hundred years before Cortez arrived to destroy it. The singular brutality employed by the Spaniards—who lacked the Aztecs' highly structured and chivalric methods of warfare—in the course of this destruction might have come as a surprise to the Mexicas, but that their empire had existed for such a short time before being taken away from them was taken more or less for granted. Cities in the Aztec mind existed largely as disposable products constructed for the temporary convenience of the gods. As long as it managed to produce sufficient turmoil to keep blood flowing into the regions of heaven and hell, a city could flourish; but any hiatus in this process would anger the gods and bring down a rain of divine wrath that could sweep a city, and civilization itself, out of existence. The Aztecs believed that just such a failure had brought the Toltecs to an end, and through their self-styled reenactment of Toltec civilization they demonstrated in astonishingly vivid ways the seriousness with which they held to this belief.

Due to the unequaled ferocity of their warriors, Tenochtitlan and its neighboring cities several times ran into the awkward situation of having run out of peoples to conquer. The prospect of peace weighed heavily on the Aztecs at these times, and they responded by inventing the "flowery war," a unique institution in which the warriors of two cities would meet at a prearranged time and place and do battle with one another solely for the purpose of obtaining sacrificial victims. These "wars," enjoyed at a distance by high-ranking spectators from the rival cities, were supervised by priests and specially designated military officials who wandered among the clusters of combatants, calling in replacements from the sidelines when appropriate. As soon as both sides felt they had accumulated enough captives to satisfy the gods, the battle was called and both "teams" trooped back to their home cities with their battered captives leading the procession. Once inside the confines of the enemy city these captives were hailed and saluted from all sides, and, provided that the prospect of imminent death on the sacrificial block had not broken their spirits they would courteously shout back their thanks at being permitted to die under such pleasant and honorable circumstances. A poem written in honor of Tlacahuepan, a particularly accomplished warrior who perished in a war between Tenochtitlan and the neighboring city of Huexotzinco, gives an example of the attitude that Aztec warriors strove to adopt toward the promise of battle—an attitude that made the field of combat a kind of momentary paradise on earth:

Banners flutter and become entangled in the field;
Like flowers the obsidian swords of death mingle together;

The chalk and the white down (of sacrifice) cause men to tremble.
Tlacahuepan was there.
O! Tlacahuepan, you came for your heart's desire—
Death by the obsidian edge of the sword.
You move about, your golden skin laced with jewels (wounds).
And so you were happy in that meadow.[29]

This poem—or song more correctly, since strictly phonetic (as opposed to hieroglyphic) writing did not arrive in Mexico until the Spaniards brought it with them—is typical of the surviving corpus of Aztec writings on warfare, both in its peculiar irony and in its equation of violent death with pleasure and ecstatic transport. Aztec songs stick to a rigid retinue of subject matter and are consistent in style and presentation. Of the several topics deemed most appropriate for celebration in song, war and sacrifice were foremost, challenged only by love and friendship—topics which, though held in great esteem, were mere trivialities in comparison to war and the rites of sacrifice that followed it.

The Aztecs loved flowers and used them constantly as metaphorical devices in their songs. Flowers are often equated with beauty and transiency in the world's literature, but in no other culture was this equation explored so thoroughly. So dense is Aztec poetry with allusions to flowers and death and the "flowery death" achieved by the warrior that this literature could be said to comprise a religion in itself—a religion that, along with its formulaic equation of death with beauty, describes an interesting exception to the general rule that the future of the disembodied human soul lay only in extinction or zombiehood. The Aztecs defined everything—people, gods, cosmic ages—by the way in which they came to an end. The Aztecs saw themselves as living in the fifth and final cosmic epoch: the sun which lit their universe was likewise the fifth and final sun, and was known by the name "Four-Movement," because this was the name of the day in the Aztec divinatory calendar when this sun would eventually be stricken from the sky by the forces of darkness and chaos. "Movement" here signifies earthquake—the specific natural catastrophe that, it was believed, would most characterize this final holocaust when it arrived. The four preceding suns or epochs were likewise known by the names of the natural disasters, such as floods or rains of fire, that had finished them.

As with ages so with individuals: the fate humans enjoyed was not determined by the evil or the good that they performed in life but rather by the circumstances in which they died. Though most of humanity was destined to end up in the wastes of the underworld, a privileged minority—drowning victims, mothers who died in childbirth—were said to go to regions of the afterlife specifically designed for them. Tlalocan, the destination of the drowned, was a simply delineated place of plenty, where there was always food to eat but about which not much else of consequence was said. The most detailed and intriguing of these parallel destinies was that enjoyed by the victims of war and sacrifice. Those killed on the field of battle or atop the temples of neighboring cities were said to avoid the frigid and hopeless realms of the underworld entirely, traveling instead to a paradise in the east, from which they would rise every morning to accompany the sun on its journey up to the roof of heaven. When the sun reached the peak of its ascent and prepared once again to endure its journey through the underworld, this group of warriors would abandon it and travel back to their home in the eastern Paradise, joining the sun once again when and if it survived the span of another night.

After four years of accompanying the sun on the pleasant portion of its daily journey, the soul of the fortunate warrior underwent a final transformation: it became a radiant bird singing forever in a fiery paradise set in some distant part of the sky exempt from that imminent catastrophe for which the rest of the Aztec universe was slated.[30] The texts describing this Paradise were taken down after the arrival of the Spaniards, who brought with them a heaven of their own, whose rules and attributes the subjected Aztecs were under tremendous pressure to adopt. But Paradise is not a Christian invention, and the version of it enjoyed by the winged spirits of the Aztec warriors bears a strong resemblance not only to the Christian Heaven but also to the flowering crown of the world tree that the shaman visits, and to which he or she conducts the souls of the newly departed once they have negotiated the maze of the underworld. It thus appears that at the time of the Conquest the Aztecs were in the process of reconstructing the shaman's ancient techniques and adapting them to the one religious practice—warfare—that could still give people the feeling that their souls partook of a reality greater than the one circumscribed by mundane, physical existence.

While the death-obsessed and war-enraptured Aztecs (and perhaps the Toltecs from whom they derived so many of their religious conceptions) might seem to have had little in common with the comparatively benign spiritual practices of the typical shamanic community, their praise of warfare and their insistence on pursuing it in spite of the crushing guilt it placed upon their civilization suggests that the whole course of Mesoamerican spiritual development—from the intimate community of the shamanic village to the chaos of metropolitan life—was about to come full circle, blossoming at last into a spiritual discipline equal to the demands of metropolitan existence. The fact that the Aztec warrior was willing to die to achieve the status of a liberated spirit is not a poetic flourish but a testament to the urgency with which these peoples were seeking an authentic experience of the soul's autonomy and power.

The ineffable condition of divinity, which religious thinkers throughout history have intuited to be the lost but potentially recoverable birthright of humanity, is, by nature of its unspeakably vivid reality, something that must be experienced concretely before it is talked about. Because the shaman was incapable of pursuing his or her fragile courtship of this state in the increasingly demanding and disorienting environment of the city—because through ignorance and neglect the underworld had become a hell devoid of transcendental promise—experience of its energies had to be accomplished through a new practice less vulnerable to the distractions of the metropolis. The Aztecs, intuiting this, refined the sacrificial practices of the Maya into a form where the act of dying itself, rather than the lineage-based "immortality" it conferred upon the killer, became the highest experience a human being could hope to achieve. While the Maya had used the shattering immediacy of violence to help give a metaphysical foundation to the chain of births and deaths by which a kingly lineage propagated itself through time, the Aztecs recognized that it was the dying individual, and not some artificially constructed "soul" made up of a chain of ancestors, who enjoyed the longed-for experience of godhood. The growth and continuation of human culture were believed more fervently by the Aztecs to have rested on the practice of warfare than they had been by any of the cultures preceding them, but this was only because they had learned their history well—a history that in Mesoamerica demonstrated both the urgent necessity of authentically experienced spirituality and the effectiveness of warfare as a provisional means to that condition of ecstasy once other methods had become lost or forgotten.

Several scholars have suggested that the Aztecs were growing so frustrated with their troublesome and costly relationship with the living gods of the earth and sky that they would eventually have been forced to abandon belief in them completely. The Aztec scholar Miguel Leon-Portilla believes that such a breakdown in mythic-religious faith was brewing at the time of the Conquest and would soon have given rise to a strictly philosophical school of thought, where concepts would take the place of gods and idols as they had done in Plato's Greece.[31] This might have been the case, but such a scenario does not explain why Aztec poetry, where Leon-Portilla finds most of his evidence for this transformation from mythos to logos, focuses so obsessively on war and bloodshed and the condition of flowery immortality achieved through it. If the Aztec elite were indeed turning away from the gods at the time of the Conquest, it would seem that they might have considered abandoning bloodshed as well, since it was presumably the gods who were forcing the practice upon mortals in the first place; but there is little indication that the thinkers of the Aztec cities had any faith in such a simple solution.

Like many writers on Mesoamerican civilization, especially Aztec civilization, Leon-Portilla occasionally falls prey to a concealed prejudice against the animistic worldview—a prejudice that reached its height in the anthropological and sociological writings of the last century and which believes this mode of experience to be nothing more than a half-baked precursor of rational thought. In fact, the experience of a world that is alive down to its smallest particle, which forms the basis for the animistic worldview, is not a perception shared only by what used to be called the "lower" cultures. Sophisticated practitioners from many of the world's most highly developed mystical traditions have described, as well as can be done with words alone, a condition of insight into the physical dimension that shows it to be far from the inert mass of dead matter in which modern consciousness feels itself to be so trapped. These practitioners have affirmed as well that access to this heightened state of perception, in which the world reveals itself as a transparent, interconnected web of living forces, cannot be attained without a modification of "normal" intelligence so violent that it can take a heavy toll on the body as well as the mind.

All across the American continent as elsewhere in the ancient world, the struggle to achieve this visionary state, while coping with the more down-to-earth problems of shelter, sustenance, and stewardship of a steadily increasing population, was capable of taking quite similar forms. Because this level of insight was so difficult to achieve, and because individuals determined to attain it used so much time and energy in the process that they were often not of much use elsewhere in the community, these native American cultures were forced early on to make decisions on how important this rarefied state was to them and how much room they were prepared to give it in the laws and customs that governed their societies. In the majority of tribes the answer to these questions was the same. Not only was the mystical condition of tremendous importance to the individuals with talent and energy enough to attain it, it was considered indispensable to the life of everyone in the community, for that realm of higher meaning was understood, even by those incapable of seeing its details in their full and sometimes terrifying clarity, to be the bedrock upon which the life of humanity was based.

To break through into this condition while alive was discovered by all who undertook it to be a tremendously dangerous task, both physically and psychologically. Along with the shamanic candidate's initiatory madness, one encounters in the native American ritual landscape a series of practices so bizarre and so damaging to the physical body that they allow one to see the often repellent and inhuman practices of the Aztecs in a slightly more charitable light. The Sioux Indians of the Central Plains of North America, one of the most culturally and metaphysically sophisticated of all the native American peoples, to this day practice rituals which involve much pain and bloodshed and which can appear to an outsider as gratuitous and masochistic. But when these practices are seen in the context of Sioux religion, they take on a very different significance. The ecstatic condition achieved in these rites is so crucial to the Sioux identity that the physical pain involved becomes for the practitioner a relatively minor aspect of the larger spiritual condition that he enters in the course of experiencing these discomforts. Pain in itself holds no great psychological or spiritual value; but when intense pain is intentionally inflicted in a sacred atmosphere it usually means that an equally intense condition of psychological insight is being sought. Three brief passages from the autobiography of Lame Deer, a modern Oglala Sioux medicine man, show how a spiritual practice involving mortifications of the body, in this case the Sioux Sun Dance, can appear from the inside:

> The dance is not so severe now as it once was, but even today it asks much of a man. Even today a man may faint for lack of food and water. He may become so thirsty blowing on his eagle-bone whistle that his throat will be parched like a cracked, dry river-bed. He may be blind for a time from staring at the sun so that his eyes see only glowing spirals of glaring whiteness. The pain in his flesh, where the eagle's claw is fastened in his breast, may become so great that a moment arrives when he will no longer feel it. It is at such moments, when he loses consciousness, when the sun burns itself into his mind, when his strength is gone and his legs buckle under him, that the visions occur—visions of becoming a medicine man, visions of the future.

> We Sioux are not a simple people; we are very complicated. We are forever looking at things from different angles. For us there is pain in joy and joy in pain, just as to us a clown is a funny man and a tragic figure at one and the same time. It is all part of the same thing—nature, which is neither sad nor glad; it just is.

> The difference between the white man and us is this: You believe in the redeeming powers of suffering, if this suffering was done by somebody else, far away, two thousand years ago. We believe that it is up to every one of us to help each other, even through the pain in our bodies. Pain to us is not "abstract," but very real. We do not lay this burden onto our god, nor do we want to miss being face to face with the spirit power. It is when we are fasting on the hilltop, or tearing our flesh at the sun dance, that we experience the sudden insight, come closest to the mind of the Great Spirit. Insight does not come cheaply, and we want no angel or saint to gain it for us and give it to us secondhand.[32]

The Aztecs were no more interested in secondhand insights than the Sioux or any of the other native American tribes. All in their own ways, and with greater or lesser degrees of success, have sought to keep the roots of human life and understanding connected to the reservoir of superhuman force on which they have intuited that the human world depends.

Because the Aztec cities were so large and complex, in terms of those daily concerns of human sustenance and government that in primitive cultures as well as modern ones take up much time and concentration, the Aztecs had no easy time of keeping the focus of the populace on the invisible world of meanings toward which a religious people must always direct itself. Consequently, their methods of keeping this larger world in mind at all times are so much more horrifying to us than the practices of cultures like the Sioux that it is all but impossible to see beyond their superficial repugnance. Yet that higher orientation is always there in Aztec ritual if one looks hard enough for it, and the outrageous forms it took as the Aztecs floundered for a better method of attaining to the company of the gods shows that the Aztecs might have had a truly remarkable future ahead of them if history had not taken the course it did.

Beauty and violence not only lived side by side in Aztec culture: through the efforts of its religious thinkers and through the highly stylized methods of war and sacrifice practiced by the state, these two disparate aspects of life were being forcibly pushed closer and closer together in order that through their paradoxical union a new view of human life and meaning could be achieved—a view that might have had more in common with the ecstatic religious practices of the Far East than with the sophists of Plato's Greece. Thanks to the Spaniards this potential union never occurred, but the outlines of its possible results can be traced not only in the Aztecs' mysteriously allusive writings on warfare but also in their stories of that "Revered Prince," Quetzalcoatl Topiltzin, who in the time of the Toltecs was said to have proclaimed the end of human sacrifice and the beginning of a new form of religious action never before practiced.

Renowned for his wisdom and holiness, Quetzalcoatl Topiltzin was, according to Aztec legend, the ideal king in the same way that Tula was the ideal city. Unconcerned with the traditional human preoccupations of lust and greed, Topiltzin lived apart from the people whose life of joy and abundance he had brought about, engaging in fasts and penitential mortifications of tremendous severity. Like the Sioux described by Lame Deer, the Aztecs held penitential acts in the highest esteem—their priests bathed regularly in frigid streams, lacerated their tongues and penises, and went without food for superhuman lengths of time. Topiltzin was remembered as the first and foremost master of all these endeavors in the same way that he was considered the father of the arts—yet according to the Aztecs these mortifications failed to satisfy the gods, who demanded nothing short of death through heart extraction in return for their sponsorship of human culture. Because of this refusal on Quetzalcoatl's part to keep up humankind's side of the bargain, the gods sent an emissary to bring Topiltzin down from greatness and the city of Tula with him.

Although most versions of the Quetzalcoatl legend dealing with the rise of Tula posit him as its founder, the later versions assert that he was a priest from a neighboring city who came to Tula after it was fully established. He brought with him a revealed doctrine preaching the worship of a "high god" who cared too deeply for mortals to go so far as to demand their deaths from them. As with the myth of the Hero Twins' descent into the underworld, these inconsistencies are the result of the longevity of the myth, which in fact was not invented outright by the Aztecs but was based to some extent on historical fact. Whether at Tula or Teotihuacan, an actual historical personage, who went under the name of Quetzalcoatl, appears to have indeed tried to stop sacrifice in favor of a new form of religious engagement. No consensus exists among scholars as to where myth ends and fact begins, but from the evidence it appears that the Tula of myth and probably of history was great both because of and in spite of sacrifice—a contradiction that the legend in its most sophisticated variants was designed to address.[33]

In all versions of the story the god Tezcatlipoca, mentioned earlier in connection with Tohil, the first god in the *Popol Vuh* to demand sacrifice from humans, is named as the chief malefactor. Like Quetzalcoatl, Tezcatlipoca took numerous forms in Aztec myth. He is present in most of their versions of the world's creation, and in general shows up wherever Quetzalcoatl himself appears, for in the Aztec mind these gods were inseparable. But whereas Quetzalcoatl's incarnations are varied and somewhat contradictory, Tezcatlipoca's are connected with a more easily identifiable complex of meanings. Whether as Moquequeloa ("The

Mocker"), Yaotl ("The Enemy"), Titlacahuan ("We are His Slaves"), or in the form of an animal avatar such as the skunk or the coyote, Tezcatlipoca was the living representative of everything in the Aztec universe that was unpredictable and threatening to human beings. Although his associations were almost entirely negative, Tezcatlipoca's character has a distinctly sophisticated "modern" flavor that is somehow appealing to twentieth-century sensibilities. The Aztecs took pains to represent this god as both all powerful and deeply scornful of humanity's petty fears and aspirations. Through him the debilitating inscrutability of human fortunes was not only accepted but given a divine standing.

Less is known about Tezcatlipoca's attributes in the cultures preceding the Aztecs, but he appears always to have been envisioned as a sorcerer or black magician of some kind—a negative manifestation of the shaman with the shaman's ability to see clearly into the past and the future. In Aztec and pre-Aztec iconography he is frequently depicted as one-legged, with that device called the "smoking mirror" where his second leg should be. In several codices a god who might be Tezcatlipoca is shown next to a watery dragon who appears to have just swallowed Tezcatlipoca's missing leg. "Smoking mirror" is sometimes translated as "talking mirror," a reference to its ability to reveal the future to those who look into its surface. By taking a few creative liberties it is thus possible to see the god's missing leg as the mark of a shamanic initiation, accomplished through an encounter with the earth-serpent, who in wounding Tezcatlipoca gives him the gift of shamanic insight. When he appears before Quetzalcoatl in Tula, he thus represents not only the vagaries of fate but also the lost shamanic spirit, returning from the realm of alienated nature to prophesy the city's doom.

Because the foibles of mortals were transparent to him and a constant source of amusement, Tezcatlipoca tends to show up in the stories of the fall of Tula in disguise, allowing the Toltecs to undo themselves with only slight intervention on his part. These stories suggest that while Tezcatlipoca appears to be the creator of this catastrophe he is actually only the emissary of a larger, frustrated force, shut off in the superhuman realms beyond the gates of human culture waiting for a chance to rush back in.

Tezcatlipoca succeeds in his onerous duties because this force he represents is both infinitely larger than the comparatively petty achievements of civilization and intimately connected with the forces of plenty that had allowed those achievements to occur in the first place. Tezcatlipoca is the emissary of this frightfully powerful force, and the tool he uses to unlock its potential in the hearts of the Toltecs is one that might be called ecstatic subversion. Two stories from the Aztec canon of myths on the fall of Tula, both translated by the American Indian scholar John Bierhorst, illustrate the method:

> It was in the middle of the market square and the sorcerer had sat down with a tiny man who danced in the palm of his hand. "I'm Master Log," he said, "and this is Huitzilopochtli [the war god of the Aztecs]."
>
> As little Huitzilopochtli danced, the people of Tula fell all over themselves to get a closer look. They pushed and shoved and trampled each other until forty were crushed to death. The next day it happened again, and the day after that. Every day forty were crushed. Finally the sorcerer said, "Toltecs, why do you put up with this? Don't be killed. Look for stones, and stone me."
>
> Without thinking, the people picked up stones and threw them at the sorcerer. They stoned him from all directions, and it wasn't long before he lay dead. But after that he began to stink. The odor was horrible, so strong that people throughout the city fainted, and many died. Wherever the wind carried the stench, people were killed.
>
> At last the dead man opened his mouth and said, "Toltecs, why do you put up with this? Don't be killed. Look for a rope, and haul me away." They found a rope and, without thinking, tied it around the sorcerer's body and began to pull. It was then that they found out how heavy he was, so heavy he couldn't be moved. They had never imagined he could weigh so much. It had never occurred to them. Well, it was time for a cry, so the crier climbed Crying Out Mound and shouted, "Toltecs, bring your heaviest log-hauling ropes and haul the dead man away."
>
> From everywhere they came running, dragging their ropes. They tied them to the sorcerer's body and started to pull, singing, "Toltecs, move. Toltecs, heave." But it wouldn't budge. They pulled harder, and when one of the ropes snapped, all the men down along the line fell on top of one another and were killed. Another rope snapped, and more men were killed. Still they were singing, "Toltecs, heave. Toltecs, move." But when the same thing had happened several times, the dead man opened

his mouth and said, "Toltecs, why do you put up with this? Don't be killed. Give me a song of my own." And he sang it for them:

> "Pull our log
> Our master
> Master log"

All together they sang the sorcerer's song, and with that the body began to move. It moved so quickly, sliding along, that whenever the Toltecs stopped to catch their breath, the dead man kept coming and would run them over, killing them by twenties and forties. When at last they had hauled him completely away, the few who were left returned to their homes without remembering what had happened. They had no idea what had been done to them. It was as if they were drunk.[34]

In the next tale Tezcatlipoca, under another disguise, announces a dance on the edge of a cliff outside the city:

> Maidens and marriageable young men came first, following close behind Tezcatlipoca as he led the way to the edge of a canyon on the outskirts of the city. Because he was a sorcerer, the people immediately did what he wanted without being told. As he struck up the beat with his drum, they started to dance, and while they danced, he composed a song, singing it out loud so that everyone could repeat the words after him.
>
> As they leaped in the air, hand in hand, their singing became a roar that could be heard from far away. This was at night, just after the sun had gone down.
>
> In the dark, as they danced, they bumped each other, pushing first one and then another over the edge of the cliff. Those who fell were killed on the crags below, and as they died they were turned into rocks. Others swarmed over the bridge that crossed the canyon. But though the bridge was of stone, the sorcerer broke it, and all the people fell on the crags. The more they danced, the more they fell. It was as though the dancing had made them drunk.
>
> The next night the Toltecs danced again. Nobody remembered what had happened the night before, and again they leaped and sang and pushed each other over the edge. Night after night they returned to the cliff, the sorcerer drumming and leading the song, and each time they danced more people were killed.[35]

Like Dionysus returning to Thebes, Tezcatlipoca here represents the old gods of nature denied—the forces of authentic divinity who cannot exist without mortals and without which mortals, whatever they decide to the contrary, can also not long survive. In both of these dramas, unfolding so far apart from each other in space and time, the behavior of these two disparate gods is oddly similar: angered by the human community's sudden retreat into hypocritical religious practices to which they are no longer invited, the gods return in disguise, unleashing here and there a devastating contagion of blind ecstatic force.[36] Overwhelmed by this returning flood of neglected energy, the people fall into trances and commit unspeakable acts from which they awake, if they awake at all, to find that their souls have turned to stone.

Whether or not they are couched in terms relating directly to human sacrifice, the nightmarish double binds encountered by civilizations losing touch with authentic forms of ecstatic communion with the divine were not a problem confined to Mesoamerica: just as all forms of human ecstasy are related and share a common root in the forces of nature out of which human consciousness grows and to which it must remain connected, so the difficulties that societies encounter in the course of their movement away from that ground take similar forms. Wandering unrecognized through the streets of Tula—just as Euripides describes Dionysus doing at Thebes—Tezcatlipoca makes use of the standard Dionysian tools of dancing, trancelike intoxication, and blind, insatiable curiosity to undo the general populace; but because the priest-king Quetzalcoatl Topiltzin is ultimately responsible for the city's having turned away from the gods by banning human sacrifice, Tezcatlipoca saves for him the form of ecstatic release that Dionysus himself most favored: sexuality.

In one such story, Tezcatlipoca again appears in the marketplace, disguised this time as a chili-pepper merchant with an unusually large penis. Quetzalcoatl in this tale is not a priest but a king who refuses to allow his chaste daughter to marry any of her numerous royal suitors. The daughter notices the naked pepper merchant and becomes inflamed with desire for him, thus causing a disastrous series of embarrassments for the king that eventually lead to his downfall. In one of the most crucial stories a group of priests, Tezcatlipoca among them, approach Quetzalcoatl Topiltzin in his quarters and show him a mirror in which he appears old and hideously disfigured. They then persuade him to take alcohol, a substance strictly forbidden to priests and penitents, and eventually succeed in getting him so drunk that he calls for his sister Quetzalpetlatl, the very embodiment of purity, and sleeps with her.

Quetzalcoatl awakes from these disastrous transgressions and departs in shame for parts unknown. Along the way he destroys all the fabulous inventions he had brought into the world for the benefit of humankind and leaves in his wake an unlikely series of landmarks that together symbolize his transit of the "cross" of the five life-directions of youth, manhood, old age, death, and finally rebirth.[37] Without him at its head, society soon goes completely to pieces. Laws are broken, human genius declines, and human sacrifice, which Topiltzin had opposed in favor of burning only snakes, birds, and butterflies, is reinstated in a last, unsuccessful attempt to appease the divine forces so outraged by its removal from humanity's program of action.

The climax of Quetzalcoatl Topiltzin's incremental journey eastward takes place on the Gulf Coast—that area of wind and waters where the first Mesoamerican cities were built and where the universe was first envisioned as a multileveled arena of shifting serpentine energies. There, on a beach bordering the celestial seas that reach out and up into the heavens, he is said to have done one of two things.[38] One source maintains that he built a raft composed of serpents and drifted off to points east, promising to return one day to banish humanity's false rulers and reinstate a higher form of existence. Another says that the priest-king built a fire on the beach and tossed himself into it, his body exploding into a crowd of birds that ascended into the sky, followed shortly thereafter by his "quetzaltototl," a Nahuatl term that translates either into "heart" or "heart of the precious penis."[39]

This ascending point of potency becomes Venus in its position as morning star, just as Hunahpu's body had done at the end of his adventures in the underworld—a celestial reference that gives an added dimension of meaning to Quetzalcoatl's eastward wanderings up to that point. Although Quetzalcoatl's banishment appears to have little in common with the twins' journey into the underworld, the two stories are in fact loosely modeled upon the same celestial scenario of the sun and the planet Venus crossing the plane of hell. But whereas in those earlier versions of this transit the "dawning" referred to by the emerging celestial bodies was an echo of the shamanic initiate's emergence into an expanded form of consciousness, the dawning here alluded to is that of ciilization itself, which through Quetzalcoatl is destroyed only to be reborn in a newer, larger form.

In all societies where the soul is taken seriously, every death is a prelude, and though on the individual level the Aztecs were growing doubtful about the soul's ability to transcend the increasingly opaque barrier of physical death, they persisted in hoping for a way out of this intolerable situation—a way whose details they had yet to formulate but which they nevertheless were eager to discover. As the embodiment of this impulse, Quetzalcoatl Topiltzin was the last and greatest hope of Aztec civilization. Though his challenge to the sacrificial tradition met with disaster, the structure of his journey eastward hints at a still-to-be-accomplished renewal—a renewal that would take the form of a spiritual discipline that could anchor the unwieldy Mesoamerican metropolis to the formative energies of the supernatural world without the essential but ultimately intolerable practice of sacrifice.

Thus, though it powered Mesoamerican civilization for centuries, sacrifice was inevitably destined to be replaced, because those centuries had left behind a suffocating residue of guilt, which in the Aztecs' experience of the world was made most obvious by the fact that those killed on the sacrificial temples were never seen or heard from again. This silence on the part of the dead invalidated the whole purpose of human sacrifice, for that tradition had grown out of earlier ones in which the spiritual candidate was dispatched to the world beyond normal experience in order to converse with and learn from the spiritual agencies who lived there. The Aztec priests dispatched—literally—an endless procession of their bravest and most beloved fellows into that region, but from it no one ever came back, bruised, burnt, or otherwise, to report to those they left behind on the mood and the character of the entities that lived there. That silence gave rise to visions of the other world as a sullen and hateful republic, crowded with souls who joined the gods in condemning humanity for its inability to communicate effectively with them.

Unless mortals are capable of entering its burning perimeters by "dying" while still alive, as the shaman and the Sioux sun-dancer does, the spiritual world becomes at worst a source of fear and at best a dimly defined catch-all for anemic philosophical speculation. Among the Aztecs it was both. Though philosophical speculation was tentatively being developed by their most accomplished thinkers, the Aztecs would probably never have found a way out of their dilemma through it, for like most American Indian cultures they had little use for truths that could not be experienced concretely. The pursuit of abstract knowledge that was not rooted in human experience did not nourish them, and until an authentic method of communion with the gods was found that did not entail the irretrievable death of the individual, they had no choice but to continue to use the battlefield and the sacrificial temple as provisional arenas for returning into their company.

All of Mesoamerican history and mythology converges upon the figure of Quetzalcoatl as he stands before the celestial sea after his banishment from Tula. It is the climax of an old drama and potentially the beginning of a new one. His entrance into the Beyond, either through immolation or by drifting off on a raft of snakes, represents a last attempt to recover the shaman's lost ecstatic abilities and transform them into a method of spiritual practice adequate for advanced, metropolitan societies. It is the place where the shaman of past generations meets the spiritual adept of future ones—the place where the human soul either enters once again into fruitful collaboration with the gods or is annihilated by them once and for all.

Tezcatlipoca himself, as the embodiment of Quetzalcoatl's destiny, hints at the shape that this last and greatest encounter between Mesoamerican mortals and the gods will take when he gives him the intoxicating beverage at Tula:

> And the old man [Tezcatlipoca] said to him then, "My prince,
> what indeed of your health?" Whereupon
> Quetzalcoatl answered, "Truly, much do I ail in
> all my parts. Nowhere am I well. My hands, my feet—
> my flesh indeed is sapped, as though it had been
> cut to pieces."

> And then the old man said, "Indeed, here is the
> potion, delicious and smooth—and it works
> within one. If you drink it, it will work in you.
> Also it will soothe your body. Also you will
> weep. Your heart will feel deserted, you will
> think upon your death. And you will think also
> upon the place where you are to go."

> Then Quetzalcoatl said, "Where am I to go, old
> one?" Then the little old man answered him,
> "Indeed, only there—toward Tollan Tlapallan—

shall you go. A man stands guard there, one
already aged. You and he shall take counsel
together. And when you return, you shall have
again been made a child."[40]

Despite their inability to court its denizens, the Aztecs had numerous names for the lost Paradise of participatory innocence, originally intuited by the shaman, where mortals, gods, and animals had enjoyed their easy kinship in the times before the Fall. Tlapallan, where Tezcatlipoca here tells Quetzalcoatl he must go, is one among several loosely designated terms for that land of perfection, and by prophesying that Quetzalcoatl will journey there and be reborn, he emerges at the end of the myth as a catalyst not only of destruction but of potential rebirth. Tlapallan is described in Aztec texts as a land of flowers and wisdom and eternal youth. The sun is born afresh from it each morning, so in terms of the planetary-shamanic scenario of descent and rebirth it can also be related to the condition of bliss and limitless vision that accompanies a successful transit of the underworld. It is also described in one source as the place where warfare was invented, which suggests that it is roughly identical to the "flowery paradise" where the souls of warriors, having undergone their fatal initiations on the field of battle, achieved their transformations into birds. The Quetzalcoatl legend ends with the specific assertion that he will one day return from this land, because the act of return is the most crucial feat performed by the shaman, and the one gesture that the flower-warrior was incapable of. Through this return, the spiritual initiate not only establishes the reality of the transhuman world but also supplies an authentic description of its character—a description that the ill-fated higher civilizations of Mesoamerica were never quite able to provide.

The Aztecs were still waiting for Quetzalcoatl to return from this eastern paradise in 1519, the year Cortez and his men emerged out of the eastern ocean bearing crosses suspiciously similar to the sign of the four cardinal directions that the god Quetzalcoatl was himself known to carry. By a very strange coincidence, 1519 corresponded to the Mexican calendar date One Reed—the year of Quetzalcoatl's birth and the year in which, it was prophesied, the god would return to humankind. Had this unfortunate conjunction of myth and history not occurred, and had the Aztecs been allowed to play out the drama of their tragically conscripted civilization to the end, might the return of Quetzalcoatl actually have taken place? Such a "return" would obviously not have taken the form of an actual personage traveling over the waves of the eastern ocean, but might instead have manifested itself as a new spiritual practice, developed by the Aztecs' priests and poets, that would have allowed the spiritual initiate to both enter into and exit from the world of superhuman force that lies beyond the gates of human culture. And if the "return" of Quetzalcoatl, carrying news of the fundamentally positive and nourishing nature of that place of renewal beyond the waters had indeed taken such a manifestation, what would the specifics of this new discipline have been?

The beginnings of an answer to these questions can be found by looking at a more successful Mesoamerican version of the journey out of the limitations of time and the contexts of everyday life and back into it—a journey routinely undertaken to this day by those same Huichol Indians of the Sierras of northwest Mexico whose shamanic huts provided a model for the origins of the Mesoamerican pyramid. Though their lifestyle is of tremendous antiquity, the Huichols themselves are relative newcomers to the lifestyle of the stationary farmer. Like the Aztecs, they appear to have descended from the same wandering groups of hunter-gatherers—known collectively as Chichimecs, or "Peoples of the Dog"—who inhabited the great stretch of desert connecting the northern interior of Mexico with the American Southwest. The Huichols' Chichimec ancestors probably adopted agricultural practices during that same infusion from the north that brought the proto-Aztecs into contact with the remnants of Toltec society. But unlike the Aztecs, the Huichols took on the constraints of an agricultural lifestyle halfheartedly. Instead of plunging into empire building and the rites of warfare and sacrifice that went with it, the Huichols never developed their agricultural techniques beyond a rudimentary level, for they appear to have sensed that along with greater material security, agriculture can bring with it a diminishment in spiritual security, for its stationary and conscripted lifestyle places the wandering hunter, already homesick for the lost but still intuited condition of Paradise, at an even greater remove from it.

The Huichols' nomadic ancestors most probably lived in a classically shamanic universe, in which every animal and plant with which they shared the earth had a spirit and personality all its own. The Huichols brought their affection for this universe with them when they took up the trappings of agriculture, and the vividness of that inheritance has made them cling to this day to the notion that things were better in the time before beans, corn, and the vortex of concerns they entail took these hunting peoples one step further away from the land of the gods.

At some point in their past, the Huichols developed a rite that allowed them to deal with this nostalgia for their previous life in a highly original and effective way: equating the first world, where mortals had been as gods, with the desert landscape that had supported their hunting ancestors, they resolved to conduct a seasonal pilgrimage to that land so that its details and the personalities who still inhabit it in the form of rocks, plants, and animals, would never be permanently lost to them. In 1966, the anthropologist Barbara G. Myerhoff accompanied a group of modern Huichols on such a journey. Although it had not remained entirely unaffected by the influences of modern civilization (part of the pilgrimage to the land of the ancestors was accomplished in a camper with the deer antlers of the Huichols' tutelary spirit strapped to the roof), the ritual elements enacted in the journey and the very real psychological transformations they accomplished for the Huichol "pilgrims" involved, convinced her that the voyage allows the Huichols to keep in touch with more than their hunting heritage: it allows them to authentically reenter the psychological landscape of Paradise, where humans, animals, and gods share a common identity.

Wirikuta, the end point of the Huichols' journey, is an unexceptional stretch of desert lying about three hundred miles east of the province of Nayarít where the modern Huichols maintain their scattered villages. Meyerhoff describes it as "a largely uninhabited, featureless brush desert of creosote and cactus,"[41] whose sacred topography often amounts to no more than a collection of oddly shaped rocks or a group of water holes. For the Huichol bands who yearly make the trek into its center, this unassuming country is experienced as if it were the very ground from which the sky and all the planets had emerged at time's inception, and the place as well where mortals were fashioned by the gods and for a time had lived with them as equals. As from Quetzalcoatl's Tlapallan, one returns from this region having again been "made as a child," for time itself evaporates in Wirikuta, human life and human meaning giving way to the topsy-turvy circumstances of eternity, where all who enter are for a moment given back the knowledge and the world-encompassing vision of the gods.

This divine condition is conferred upon the Huichols before they set out for Wirikuta through a series of ritualized transformations, in the first of which the shaman gives each pilgrim the name of one of the Huichols' many gods, which he or she will "become" for the duration of the voyage. For several days before the journey begins, the Huichol pilgrim is made to focus attention upon himself or herself as an eating, drinking, sleeping, speaking, fornicating creature—a human being with human habits that must be either radically altered or stopped altogether before the journey into godhood can begin. Like Quetzalcoatl, who scatters his human riches on the winds or has them robbed from him (depending on the version) on the way to Tlapallan, the Huichol pilgrims gradually learn to leave behind the human habits and attributes that define them in their daily world. By the time they arrive at Wirikuta they partake of a condition that is both familiar and immeasurably strange, for it is the condition that all humans had once enjoyed before they left it behind with their descent into culture. The shaman in charge of the journey works to intensify this feeling of disorientation all along the way into the sacred landscape. For example, after passing a certain point in the journey the pilgrims, already dazed from lack of food and sleep, are no longer permitted to converse with one another in normal terms but must speak instead through "the reversals," a modified form of communication in which one says the opposite of what one means.

Because Wirikuta is considered to be the womb of the world and of creation, the landmarks at its outskirts have decidedly feminine names. The first threshold that the pilgrims pass through is called, literally, "the vagina" and corresponds roughly to the river of clashing knives on the edge of Xibalba. Here, at this typically shamanic point of entrance into the realm beyond the ordinary mortal plane, newcomers to the journey are blindfolded and remain so for the short journey to another station point called "where the mothers dwell," the first landmark entirely within the boundaries of the sacred world, which Myerhoff describes as "a dozen little dirty puddles, a series of permanent springs beside a small marsh, punctuated by a solitary stunted tree."[42] Ramón, the shaman in charge of Myerhoff's expedition, had so carefully orchestrated the pilgrims' experiences up to this point that here, at this unspectacular collection of water holes, they were made to "see" the country before them as the first humans had seen it—limitless, uncanny, and filled with half-remembered details of the world as it had been when humans had walked upon it as gods. Here is Myerhoff's description of the event:

> The *peyoteros* [pilgrims] assembled in a line, in their proper order, facing the ever-brightening eastern sky while Ramón chanted, prayed, and gestured with his plumes, until he directed them to set down their bundles. Ramón, at the head of the line, then beckoned forward the first pilgrim, Carlos. Ramón squatted beside the largest water hole and taking up some in his gourd bowl removed Carlos' hat and poured water into it. He then touched both of Carlos' eyes with his plumes, sprinkled water on his head, and had him drink that remaining in the bowl. The ritual varied somewhat for the *primeros* [blindfolded newcomers]. Ramón took more time and care with them, praying over them longer. After they had drunk the Sacred Water instead of sending them immediately back to their places in line he removed their blindfolds and urged them to gaze up and behold the sacred place to which they had returned as gods. He pointed out the important features of the landscape, the places the gods had stopped and rested, eaten, sung, or talked with the animals while traveling back to their homeland. Especially affecting were Ramón's ministrations over Lupe [Ramón's wife—a newcomer to the peyote pilgrimage] at this time. He carefully led her from her place to the water and she remained motionless for a moment after he had removed her blindfold. He bade her to lift her eyes, to behold the place of the Ancient Ones, where it all began, and she did so slowly, almost reluctantly. The sun struck her face fully. She seemed transfixed and tears spread evenly down the wrinkles of her rapturous face. Seeing her thus no one could help but know that she found the Sacred Land to be as beautiful as she had been told all her life. Ramón grasped her arm and led her back to the line with apparent satisfaction; all was as he had said. He had brought her here safely, and that she was his wife and so moved by the experience which he had made possible for her unquestionably intensified the meaning of the moment for both of them.[43]

This first glimpse of Paradise is followed by a penetration to its very center, a field of scrub and cactus where the pilgrims are led by the shaman on a "hunt" for peyote, that unassuming-looking cactus whose hallucinogenic properties have played such a large part in the religious life of the Indians of the American Southwest.

The Huichols identify peyote with their most sacred animal—the deer—which in times past was both their primary source of food and their chief connection to the legions of animals with whom they shared the desert. The pilgrims "stalk" the small, pincushion-shaped plant exactly as if it were a deer itself, creeping cautiously across the scrubland of Wirikuta until a growth of it is spotted, at which point the shaman creeps slowly up and shoots two sacred arrows through its base, one in an east-west direction and one in a north-south direction. This axis symbolizes the center of the world, and the peyote itself thus becomes for a moment a model of that tree whose roots and trunk unite the three cosmic zones. Though physically the peyote is an unlikely candidate for the world tree, the changes in perception it creates when eaten make the unity of earth, heaven, and hell an experiential reality for the Huichols, who therefore venerate it as a giant growing among them.

Once the "kill" has been made the shaman uses a set of feathers to brush the multicolored lines of energy—visible only to him—that the arrows have jolted out of the top of the plant back down into its center. This first kill is followed by a more general harvest of the area, after which the pilgrims depart with the collected cacti stacked carefully in special baskets designed to make their journey out of Wirikuta a comfortable one. Individual peyote plants are treated much as if they were themselves tiny Huichols: their anatomy is described in human terms and it is taken for granted that they are able to hear and understand all that is said and done around them. Anxious not to offend any of the plants taken on the hunt, the pilgrims speak individually to each of them, thanking them for their sponsorship of the human community and assuring them that their "bones" (roots) will be left behind in Wirikuta so that they may successfully resurrect themselves in the coming year.

Once back in the Huichol village, the stored peyote is used casually and in rituals throughout the year, the mild hallucinations and altered sense of identity that it produces being taken advantage of by the Huichols in much the same way that our society uses alcohol. Though the changes in human perception that peyote brings about are more radical than those produced by alcohol, the Huichol lifestyle is itself so permeated with the flavor of the uncanny that frequent ingestion of the plant serves not to subvert or corrupt that lifestyle but instead to validate it. By our standards, all of Huichol life is a kind of well-organized hallucination, for the cosmos they believe and live in bears very little resemblance to the one that Western civilization wakes up to every morning. The enormous part that the visionary condition plays in Huichol culture is not maintained without a great deal of effort and caution, however, and has resulted in an intricate set of rules regarding the spirit world whose forces enter so pervasively into daily Huichol life. Tezcatlipoca's catastrophic ecstasies are not unknown to the Huichols, but because these negative forms of consciousness make up no more than a portion of the superhuman energies that their society is structured to be in such close and constant communication with, the Huichols are not unduly frightened of them, believing them to attack only those individuals whose psyches are unbalanced in the first place.

Though the Southwestern desert supports a number of potent hallucinogenic plants, the Huichols use only a specific variety of peyote to achieve visions, for they believe the other hallucinogenic species harbor deceitful spirits who can seduce one into committing horrendous errors of action and judgment. A person who has defied the wishes of the gods and of his or her fellows by ingesting the wrong species of hallucinogen—or even "good" peyote under the wrong conditions—can labor under various destructive ecstatic transports, such as mistaking one of the giant cacti that grow in the deserts thereabout for a beautiful woman and fornicating with it, a trick that Tezcatlipoca might have tried on the Toltecs had he known about it.

Wirikuta itself is as dangerous and potentially damaging a place as the uncultivated deserts that surrounded Tula and the Aztec cities, and must be approached with caution and under proper ritual conditions, or it too will unhinge the psyche—and it is just such catastrophic transports that the intricate series of behavior alterations undergone by the pilgrims prior to their journey are designed to prevent. It is only by taking such care in establishing their relationship with Wirikuta, and by acknowledging the negative manifestations of the forces that live there, that the Huichols have succeeded in making their simple farming communities into stations on the very edge of Paradise. By appraising the human condition in the light of the state of unconditional grace that preceded it, the Huichols have come to regard the human body as a garment to be discarded and reassumed at will, so that the limits it imposes can never be mistaken for the totality of experience and the desires to which it is prone are not taken as ends in themselves but rather as passage points into the condition of godhood.

Though Wirikuta differs from the typical shamanic landscape in that it is an actual, physical locality on the surface of the earth instead of somewhere beneath or above it, and though the shaman is capable of visiting it not only in trance but physically, the body he and his charges bring with them on their pilgrimages is not the same as the "fallen," mortal body, subject to hunger, thirst, disease, and death, that they experience in daily life. This mortal body is in essence left behind in the village. This twist on the standard shamanic method shows that successful ecstatic states do not have to involve an actual separation of the soul from the body but can instead take place when the body itself is remade to temporarily conform to the laws of the spirit. This is in fact what happens in the Sun Dance. The body there is pushed to the absolute limits of its endurance; it is made to dance on the edge between the human and the supernatural worlds until physical exhaustion draws the dancer back into the normal, physically embodied state in which humans carry out the business of love and hatred, misery and happiness—pursuits that, in their limited and clumsy way, are just as valid as the eternal and infinitely graceful endeavors of the gods.

For the Huichols, the beauty and brilliance of the supernatural world is not a cause for shame arising from unfortunate comparisons with their present state so much as it is a perennial comfort and inspiration. Like a group of children watching from a distance as a group of adults play with coordination and supreme confidence a game whose rules and demands are for the moment slightly beyond their capacities, the Huichols keep their eyes on Wirikuta from a distance, looking to it for guidance and wandering back, at times, into its midst. At such times they wear the costumes and don the mannerisms of the gods in as competent a manner as possible. If they are careful in this pantomime, they attain for a moment that overpowering and invaluable sensation, achieved in various ways by various peoples across the earth since the beginnings of history, that the seat of their identity shares in that same inexhaustible condition of grace that the gods themselves enjoy.

Descending from this brief flirtation with the gods of the primordial land of Origins, these Huichol emissaries from the makeshift world of human life and human disappointments wander back, thoroughly exhausted, to resume their roles as men and women in that community just west of Paradise that, for the moment, they call their home. There they go about their human business, and plan to do so until that day, far in the future, when the human and the divine worlds will once more become one.

In Mesoamerica as elsewhere in the ancient world, architecture was designed to reflect spiritual topography. Though both the Huichols and the Aztecs built their towns and cities in the hope that they would function as cosmic centers, both knew that until humanity reattained the condition of divinity lost in the Fall into culture, any physical manifestation of that culture would inevitably be slightly askew. Hence both cultures postulated a land apart from the human community where the true axis lay—a land that the Huichols, but not the Aztecs, managed to enter into momentary contact with. For the Huichols, these brief moments of participation in the world of Origins turn out to be enough to make their present, merely human state, not only bearable but joyous. "You have seen how it is when we walk for the peyote," the shaman Ramon said to Myerhoff. "How we go, not eating, not drinking, with much hunger, with much thirst. With much will. All of one heart, of one will. How one goes, being Huichol. That is our unity, our life."[44] It is a life which, Ramon has said elsewhere with unforced matter-of-factness is beautiful because it is right.

These words, so similar in their way to Lame Deer's defense of the Sun Dance, show once again that in the Indian universe the ostensible goals achieved in ritual ordeals, such as the attainment of food or sacred plants, are often secondary to the psychological transformations undergone by the voyager in the course of the journey. The Huichol pilgrims leave the land of Origins with more than just a year's supply of peyote: they leave with proof of Wirikuta's sponsorship. As with the Eskimo shaman's visit to the Mother of the Sea Beasts, the Huichols' shamanic journey to Wirikuta is really undertaken to ensure that the lines of communication between mortals and gods stay strong enough for the drawbacks of the human condition to be seen in perspective. Of all of Mexico's broken and subjugated native peoples, the Huichols alone have remained, at least until recently, truly aloof to outside impacts—a feat that could not have been accomplished, through the long centuries of bullying and spiritual coersion, without the benefit of an energy, a source of inspiration beyond the limited strengths derived from simple cultural pride. This reservoir of strength is Wirikuta itself, the storehouse of superhuman energy and insight, portions of which, every year, are brought back by the pilgrims in the form of well-packed peyote plants, to their fellows living in the world of human life and human contradiction.

As important as peyote is to the Huichol lifestyle, the real treasure attained by the Huichol peyote pilgrims and by all ecstatic voyagers into realms beyond the human sphere—the force that allows them and their community to put up with almost anything that the world of daily life throws at them—is proof of membership among the gods through an authentic experience of the individual soul's own eternal nature. In Aztec times the warrior elite discovered in the rarefied atmosphere of combat a similar feeling of undying fellowship with the universe: a feeling that these warriors expressed by saluting each other as "brother" or "nephew," even as they sought to cut each other to pieces, and by likening themselves, in their postmortem condition, to radiantly feathered birds.

Huichol children are introduced early to the mysteries of the peyote hunt through a narrative called "When the Mara'akame [the Huichol term for the shaman] Plays the Drum and Flies the Children to the Land of Peyote." This tale is told to the children by the shaman himself, who before commencing with it asks the children to imagine everything he tells them very clearly, because in truth they will not remain where they are sitting but will travel out of themselves, strung behind the shaman like a group of birds. The children are instructed to "act and feel like eagles," because the place to which they are traveling is dangerous and will swallow them into itself if they do not keep their wits about them. Flying over the sacred landscape that they will perhaps visit later as adults, the bird-children alight on one after another of the sacred landmarks leading to the heart of Wirikuta. Once there the children are introduced to the divine Ancestors for the first time and the shaman speaks to these Ancestors on behalf of the children:

> "Oh, Our Father, Our Grandfather, Our Mothers, you all who dwell here, we have arrived to visit you, to come and see you here. We have arrived well." And when they arrive, they kneel and Our Father, Our Grandfather, Our Elder Brother, embrace them.
>
> "What did you come for, my children?" they ask. "You have come so far, why did you travel so far?"

> They answer, "We came to visit you so that we will know all, so that we will have life."
>
> "All right," they say, "it is well," and they bless them. And there they remain but ten minutes, a very few minutes, to speak with Our Father, Our Grandfather, with all of them there. And then the Mother gives them the blessing and they leave.[45]

Arriving back in their village, the children are congratulated by the shaman for performing well on the journey and each is given a miniature tortilla, which he instructs them to show around to their relatives as proof of their first successful journey out of human life and into Wirikuta, whose blessings they have now received and which they will carry with them for the rest of their lives.

A tremendous distance separates this humble but formative journey, experienced by every Huichol youngster, from the horrific details of the Aztec dramas of sacrifice and warfare. Yet the place to which the winged Aztec warrior and the winged Huichol child travel is in essence the same. Whether it is known as Wirikuta, Tlapallan, or by any of the thousand other names that have been given it over the centuries, this region has served as a focus of human longings and an impetus for human actions—both coherent and misdirected—that in Mesoamerica at least had a surprisingly consistent part to play in the unfolding of that region's history. Heaven, Paradise—these are entirely exhausted words to us, and it is difficult to understand or sympathize with a people who would take them or their equivalents seriously. Yet both the stubborn contentment of the Huichols and the legendary restlessness of the Aztecs were largely the result of their relationships with such places. It was to this realm of abundance and potential destruction that the poets and philosophers of late Aztec times directed an unanswered chorus of questions, pleas, and salutations, and which they sent Quetzalcoatl, through the agency of myth, to explore and recover for them. When the Aztecs looked around them and decided that everything in the universe was destined to wind down, when they postulated that the sun—the star beneath the earth, which is actually human life and human consciousness itself—would one day be extinguished in the belly of the night, they did so with their own, inchoate dreams of paradise in mind.

The solution for the Aztecs, and the solution for any society so lost in itself that it has crowded out the greater realities of the spirit, is spiritual practice capable of delivering an authentic experience of humankind's divinity. The possibility for such a practice lay both in the mass of mythic fragments that the Aztecs had gathered from the civilizations that had preceded them as well as in their own half-formulated desire for the promise of a life beyond the body.

It is not our purpose to press the point, but in terms of their ambivalence about the physical world and the other world that might or might not lie in wait behind it, the spiritual situation of the fifteenth-century Aztecs was a good deal closer to our own than we would perhaps like to imagine. It is true that the Aztecs believed in a pantheon of gods that we claim to have outgrown, but beyond the terms in which they are couched our fundamental fears and insecurities have much in common. With that in mind, let us take a closer look at this people as they flailed about in search of a path beyond the limitations of physicality and mortality, and at the rites of violence and bloodshed that, in their flawed and costly way, supported them as they waited for Quetzalcoatl to return with the feathered legions of the sacrificial dead strung out behind him.

3

The Hazardous World

▼▼

The hidden world has its clouds and rain, but of a
      different kind.
   Its sky and sunshine are of a different kind.
   This is made apparent only to the refined ones—those
      not deceived
by the seeming completeness of the ordinary world.

Jalaludin Rumi

Insofar as he is spirit it is man's misfortune to have the
body of an animal and thus to be like a thing, but it is
the glory of the human body to be the substratum of a
spirit. And the spirit is so closely linked to the body as a
thing that the body never ceases to be haunted, is never a
thing except virtually, so much so that if death reduces it
to the condition of a thing, the spirit is more present than
ever: the body that has betrayed it reveals it more clearly
than when it served it. In a sense the corpse is the most
complete affirmation of the spirit.

Georges Bataille
Theory of Religion

8. *The Aztec earth goddess Cihuacoatl, with mouth agape to show her perpetual hunger for human sacrificial victims. This post-Conquest illustration by an Aztec artist appears in Durán's* Book of the Gods and Rites. *(Redrawn by the author.)*

F IVE HUNDRED YEARS AGO, the valley in the Central Highlands that today struggles to support the ever-growing sprawl of Mexico City was known by the picturesque name of Anahuac, or "By the Waters." Nothing remains of the brackish lake that took up much of the valley's base at this time, but it was this lake and the wildlife it supported that originally attracted Indian settlers to the area. In comparison with the lands surrounding it, Anahuac in these times was an oasis whose surrounding forests and fields were as thick with deer and partridge as the lake was with ducks, fish, and other edible fare. The soil was rich and capable of supporting corn and beans to feed a relatively dense population, while five surrounding snow-capped mountains gave the area an atmosphere of centrality, as if the gods had constructed them intentionally to frame a human community. To the north and east lay the ruins of Teotihuacan; to the north and west the more recently abandoned Toltec city of Tula lay as a promise and a warning of things to come.

It was into this valley that the half-dozen hunting tribes who were to develop into the civilization we know as the Aztecs descended in the years following Tula's collapse. Hunters and wanderers by tradition, these Chichimec groups had for centuries led a spare but vigorous existence under the aegis of tribal gods, who traveled with their devotees in the form of crude wooden images wrapped in the skins of animals. The individual flavor of life in the wastes of "Godland," as the northern deserts were called by their peoples, is difficult to recapture because few clues about it exist in the archaeological or anthropological records. Like most hunting peoples, they did not feel the need to leave much documentation of themselves behind, preferring to focus their attentions on the precarious rhythms of the land and the beings, visible and invisible, that moved across it with them. It would be convenient to be able to say that these archaic tribes lived in peaceful coexistence with one another—the better to contrast this portion of their history with the disturbing events that came later—but from the limited evidence available it appears that they were a fairly rough bunch even before they entered into the arena of metropolitan existence. The occasional human sacrifice was not unknown to them, and their essentially aggressive character is evidenced by the speed with which they took over the lands to the south after Tula's defenses had broken down from the inside.[1]

The last of these nomadic groups to abandon the northern desert for the stationary life of plenty in Anahuac was called the Mexica, possibly in reference to Mecitli, or "Grandmother Maguey," an early Chichimec version of the ominous Aztec Earth Mother. Like the tribes who had come to the lake before them, the Mexica believed themselves to have emerged at some point in the mythic past from Azatlan—yet another version of the cosmically orienting "Place of Seven Caves"—from which the Aztecs as a whole receive their name; and like those fellow tribes, they were now determined to trade in the wandering lifestyle they had known for centuries for the richer but strangely problematic world of the urban agriculturalist.

Much of what has been written about "the Aztecs" relates most specifically to the Mexica, for in addition to being the best-documented of all the Aztec tribes, they were the most instrumental in transforming the largely Toltec-derivative style of life in Anahuac in the years after Tula's fall into the uniquely twisted spectacle that Cortez was to encounter a scant two hundred years later.[2] The Mexica took the game of kingship and empire that had been played for over a thousand years in Mesoamerica and brought it to life with such sincerity that with them as with no other people before them the true motivations that lay behind the Mesoamerican metropolitan tradition become apparent—if not entirely to the Mexica themselves, at least potentially for us.

Sacrificial warfare on a grand scale had been taken up by the Mexica's Aztec predecessors at Lake Tezcoco—as this body of water was known to its Indian inhabitants—more or less as a matter of course. By the time this last, seemingly insignificant band of nomads reached the shores of the lake in the early fourteenth century, the several tribes that had preceded them there had already established themselves in the choicest spots along the shore, intermingling with the remaining Toltec stock and learning from them the etiquette of the perpetual warfare in which any self-respecting Mesoamerican city was expected to indulge. Few in number, ignorant of farming techniques, and in any case lacking their own land to farm even if they had possessed the necessary skills, the Mexica established themselves on a small, unclaimed area on the lake's western shore near a natural landmark called the Rock of Chapultepec and immediately astonished their haughty and well-established neighbors by audaciously raiding their food and weapon supplies and dragging off their women in order to more rapidly increase their numbers.

The Mexica spent about three decades at Chapultepec, gradually gaining proficiency in the crafts of a sedentary people and learning how to get sustenance from the flora and fauna of Tezcoco's rich waters. But their persistent harassment of the larger settlements to the north and south of them eventually prompted a merciless group attack that decimated their numbers overnight. Culhuacan, a city on Tezcoco's southern shore with a particularly prestigious Toltec heritage, was instrumental in the massacre, capturing the Mexica's then-leader Huitzilihuitl and dragging him, his wife, and their children back to Culhuacan to be sacrificed. According to the sketchy native documentation of this incident, Huitzilihuitl's people were already held in such low esteem by Culhuacan and the other lakeshore cities that both he and his family were forced to undergo the tremendous indignity of being sacrificed naked—an insult far more offensive than the act of sacrifice itself, which was by this time a commonplace in the burgeoning cultural world of Anahuac.

During the attack, some of the Mexica had run blindly into the lake to escape death, and some of these eventually congregated just off the western shore on a reedy sliver of land that up until then had been populated only by frogs, nesting waterfowl, and mosquitoes. Naked, shelterless, and with most of their hunting equipment left behind with the bodies of their murdered fellows, this handful of refugees was only slightly worse off than those few of their fellows back on land that the attackers had not had the energy or inclination to kill. This second contingent of survivors was established on an equally miserable stretch of land called Tizapan, which lay next to Culhuacan on the southern shore of the lake and which had remained empty of people up to that point because of the uncommonly large population of poisonous snakes it supported. Under the mistaken impression that this second portion of survivors had been sufficiently terrorized by the attack to no longer constitute a significant threat, Culhuacan allowed them to make do as best they could on this snake-infested stretch of rocky shoreline, while exacting a heavy tribute of labor from them and generally taking pleasure at the state of humility these troublesome newcomers had been forced to accept.

Ever ready to adapt to the rigors of a new situation, this group is said to have foiled the plans of their new masters by rapidly devouring all the snakes in the area and quickly recovering enough of their already legendary lust for war to be useful in the various campaigns that Culhuacan was waging against its neighbors. Before long, the unprecedented bravado demonstrated by these Mexica warriors so impressed the Culhuacan nobility that the strictures imposed upon them were relaxed and the two peoples began to intermarry. Culhuacan was said to have had—along with its largely Chichimec population—many individuals who carried in their veins the pure blood of the greatly idealized Toltecs, those masterful culture-creators who under Quetzalcoatl Topiltzin had produced all the brilliant creations of metropolitan civilization that the Chichimec newcomers were now striving so hard to reproduce. This commingling of bloodlines gave the Culhuacan Mexicans a hereditary connection to the Toltecs that they would make much of in the years to come, and brought them on their first major step toward cultural legitimacy.

At this point in their development, the Aztec peoples were not very different from any other nouveau riche community: seduced by the splendor and novelty of an alien way of life, they were doing everything possible to disavow their previous traditions and assume the postures and motions of the newly discovered system. Peoples who for centuries had lived in nothing much larger than tents and who depended for leadership on individuals chosen for their cunning or their abilities with the supernatural world were now speaking with disdain of the "barbarian" races while constructing lofty temples for their improved, urban-agricultural deities and their ever-increasing political and religious nobility.

The Mexica were as eager to stake their claim in this new metropolitan universe as any of their fellows and possibly more so, but to the eyes of the already established Chichimec-Toltec cities there was something disturbing about the fury with which they were going about establishing that claim. In the years they had spent at the Rock of Chapultepec they had managed to become the subjects of a deep-seated hatred among all the peoples of the lake, and there were apparently members of the Culhuacan nobility who viewed their acceptance into Culhuacan society with deep misgivings.

Like all the tribes that had wandered down out of the desert and set up along the lake, the Mexica had a tribal god, a tutelary deity whose bundled image was tended by protopriests to whom he spoke his desires, in more or less shamanic fashion, at night as they dreamed. While the other cities on the lake had at some point exchanged their Chichimec deities for gods with very ancient pedigrees such as Quetzalcoatl or Tezcatlipoca, the god of the Mexica was a unique creation. His name was Huitzilopochtli, the "Hummingbird from the South," and we saw him in the last chapter dancing in the palm of Tezcatlipoca during his bewitchment of the people of Tula.[3] Like Tezcatlipoca and the majority of the Aztecs' other gods, Huitzilopochtli possessed few humane or reassuring qualities; the well-being of humans was of little concern to him and the only reason he favored the Mexica was, in their view, because he knew that they would one day command the greatest city in the world, which through diligent pursuit of battle would keep a steady supply of blood flowing up into the heavens. The statement of the crazed drill sergeant in Stanley Kubrick's film *Full Metal Jacket* that God "has a hard-on for Marines [because] they keep heaven packed with fresh souls" comes surprisingly close to summarizing Huitzilopochtli's reasons for sponsoring the Mexica. Indeed, the entire atmosphere of that film, in which young men are depicted committing perverse acts of violence in response to a dimly articulated but convulsively felt allegiance to the power of death, is very similar to the atmosphere one gets from the myth and history of Huitzilopochtli's Mexica. Legend states that Huitzilopochtli had taken the Mexica under his wing at just that point in their history when they had given up their desert wanderings to pursue the life of the city. Before then this tribe had worshiped an earth goddess with the character and skills of a shaman-sorceress, about whom little is said except that she had been Huitzilopochtli's sister and that he, disapproving of her methods, had encouraged the Mexica to abandon her in the deserts and follow him south into the world of Anahuac.

The Mexica's audacious behavior at Chapultepec had largely been the doing of Huitzilopochtli. Through his priestly mouthpieces he had badgered the Mexica to be quick about establishing themselves in a stationary place so that they might build a temple to him and from that station set about conquering all the world in his name. As well as being the brother of the spurned sorceress-goddess of the deserts, Huitzilopochtli was said to be the son of another earth goddess, Coatlique, who had given birth to him fully armed and ready for warfare. In his incessant demands for war and the blood of sacrifice, Huitzilopochtli thus spoke not only for himself but for all the zombielike gods of the newly refurbished, Aztec version of the Mesoamerican metropolitan universe, who allowed humans to exist only so long as they produced these spectacles for the gods' enjoyment and sustenance.

Huitzilopochtli's wooden idol had been taken from the Mexica by Culhuacan in the massacre at Chapultepec, but as relations between the two peoples improved it was decided that this cherished object would be given back to them and that they should be allowed to construct a temple where he could be appropriately venerated. Overjoyed at once again possessing the image of their supernatural mentor, the Mexica produced a temple for him in short order and held an opening ceremony for it involving the sacrifice of several victims they had managed to collect in the course of their battles for Culhuacan. Though the Culhua were well acquainted with the dogma of sacrifice as a means of increasing a city's prestige in the eyes of the gods, they do not seem to have derived the same crazed satisfaction from it that the Mexica did: upon witnessing the frenzied proceedings that attended the opening of Huitzilopochtli's temple, many of the Culhua became convinced that their Mexican subjects were dangerously imbalanced and that no matter how useful they might be as warriors, their presence constituted a threat to the city's well-being. A quarrel broke out between those who thought the Mexica too valuable to let go of and those who thought they were a dangerous and offensive band of lunatics. The latter faction prevailed and set with clubs and spears upon the Mexica, who for the heat of their devotion to their god found themselves once again dashing helter-skelter into the waters of the lake.

The trouble had erupted so suddenly that they were given no time to assemble their belongings or prepare canoes but were forced instead to swim for it. Carrying little in the way of supplies, but at least in possession of the all-important idol of Huitzilo-pochtli, the beleaguered survivors of this second rout swam out toward the marshy bog where their fellows had been struggling to survive since the day the two groups had been separated at Chapultepec. Next to that first island where their fellows had reluctantly settled lay another, equally small and equally inhospitable, called Tenochtitlan, because numerous tenochtli cacti grew there. The fruit of the tenochtli cactus is red, and is roughly the size and shape of the human heart. According to legend Huitzilopochtli let his subjects know that they had at last found the spot where he wished his city to be built by placing on one of these cacti an eagle with a writhing serpent grasped in its beak—an image that became the symbol both of human sacrifice and the uncontested supremacy of its Mexica practitioners and which survives to this day as the national seal of Mexico.

Whether or not such an eagle was actually awaiting the Mexica who staggered out of the water with those Culhuacan husbands and wives who had chosen to defect with them, this people's inexplicably stubborn vision of the glorious destiny that awaited them remained untainted, and they accepted their new homeland with a characteristic lack of regard for the odds against their continuing survival. Surrounded on all sides by large, well-fed cities who could have wiped them out if they cared to expend the effort, they quietly began assembling the first reed structures of what, in just over a century's time, would become the greatest city in Mesoamerica, with palaces, extensive suburbs, and a population of somewhere over half a million souls. Following the example of their neighbors on the adjoining spit of land that would eventually develop into the suburb-city of Tlatilulco, the Culhuacan Mexica dredged up mud from the surrounding waters and spread it over bound bales of water weeds, creating artificial, floating gardens, or chinampas, from which they soon were able to coax a limited but valuable amount of food crops. Fish, frogs, waterfowl, and various "cheeses" made from compacted fish and insect eggs or algae scraped from the surface of the lake were among the food items that sustained them during these difficult times. As if the task of building a settlement entirely from scratch on a patch of mud within eyeshot and easy reach of their numerous enemies were not enough, the Mexica now had to cope with the problem of securing drinking water, which was all but nonexistent on the islands themselves. Intrepid boatmen daily risked their lives sneaking over to freshwater springs on the mainland, loading down their canoes, and paddling back to the twin islands, which month by month grew larger both in population and in surface area.

Once again, the surrounding cities made the mistake of believing the Mexica's and the Tlatilulcans' situation to be so bad that they didn't take the effort to crush them while they still had the chance. After a few years had passed and it was realized that, against all probability, the Mexica were not withering away on their island refuges but were transforming them into viable and productive communities, tentative communications were again established between the two islands and the more powerful cities on the lake's western shore, which once more began using the Mexica's suicidally intrepid warriors on their various arbitrary campaigns and harassments.

Lake Tezcoco had for some time been politically divided roughly down the middle, with the cities on the western bank, known broadly as the Tepaneca, squabbling perpetually with those on the eastern bank, which were known collectively as the Acolhua. In the decades following their settlement of the twin islands of Tenochtitlan and Tlatilulco, the Mexica learned how to exploit their position at the center of these tensions to their advantage, lending their services to whichever city offered the greatest strategic possibilities at that particular moment. These intrigues climaxed early in the fifteenth century with the formation of the Triple Alliance, a revolutionary partnership between Tenochtitlan and two powerful lakeside cities—Tlacopan and Tezcoco—that allowed these three to achieve undisputed mastery of Anahuac and the lands surrounding it for many miles.

Tlacopan lay on the western side of the lake with Tezcoco across from it, and the now very substantial island city of Tenochtitlan perched directly in between. So great was the combined strength of their warriors that effective resistance on the part of the other cities in the region, to whom the idea of grouping together as a united front had never occurred, became impossible. As a result the marketplaces of Tenochtitlan and Tlatilulco began to receive a flood of food, human labor, and luxury goods from the various cities now under their dominion. Accustomed until recently to foraging for frogs and salamanders and scraping insect larvae from the surface of the lake, the Mexica now found themselves glutted with such items as conch-shell trumpets from the Gulf Coast, elaborate quetzal feather headdresses from the fringes of Maya country far to the south, gold and jade both worked and unworked, and as much free labor as they chose to demand from the cities and towns surrounding them.

It would have taken comparatively little effort for the Mexica to keep their newfound opulence intact for some years to come, and one might expect this rush of worldly pleasures to have softened their troublemaking tendencies. But such was not the case, for despite their increasing political sophistication, the Mexica continued to see war not as a means to an end but as an end in itself. Instead of strategically loosening their stranglehold on the peoples surrounding them just enough to avoid the possibility of mass revolt, they tightened it beyond endurance. Subject cities might be pressed to deliver such absurdly large amounts of tribute items that they had no choice but to refuse. Once given this excuse for battle, the Mexica would send a messenger off to the offending town or city, alerting it with strangely inappropriate courtesy of the date on which it could expect a troop of Mexican warriors to arrive. Depending on the Mexica's mood, such cities might only suffer the loss of some of their warriors or they might instead be crushed completely, their temples and their habitations razed, their men murdered on the sacrificial block, and their women and children scattered across the countryside or sold into slavery. The godly injunction of war for war's sake continued to be taken with absolute and unwavering seriousness by the Mexica's rulers, who though they were now at the head of a politically and economically complex empire continued to act with the same crazed intensity as they had in the days when they were a ragged group of wanderers carrying the image of their tribal god about in search of their destined homeland.

Huitzilopochtli's image was now installed at the center of the Temenos, an imposing temple structure at the heart of Tenochtitlan from which causeways led out through the crowded streets and canals of the city and across the waters of the lake. The dedication of this temple occurred in 1455 and took over four days to accomplish. Over twelve thousand victims were sacrificed at its summit during this time, making it far and away the largest recorded sacrificial ritual in the history of Mesoamerica. Leaders of every city for miles around were invited to witness the event, including those that had somehow managed to elude Mexican domination thus far. These enemy rulers were treated with special courtesies, and after they had finished witnessing hundreds of their captured comrades die atop the hundred-foot temple, they were heaped with gifts and seen safely back out to the limits of the city. Yet in spite of all these efforts on his behalf, Huitzilopochtli re-

9. *Huitzilopochtli's temple within the Temenos,
the sacred center of Tenochtitlan, as depicted
by a European artist.*

mained as impatient with his chosen people as ever, and no matter
how great the number of souls his subjects sent into the heavens,
he continued to crave more.

Burr Cartwright Brundage, who has written the only comprehensive modern treatment of the Mexica's confused and tumultu-
ous history, repeatedly makes the point that unlike other ancient
warlike states, the Aztec cities in general and the Mexica's particularly were always far more concerned with the activity of war
itself than with the rewards it produced. It is this single-minded
devotion to the practice, which did not fade in intensity with their
growing wealth and influence but instead grew ever stronger and
was ever more desperately pursued, that shows the Mexica Aztecs
to be one of the most uniquely preoccupied civilizations the world
has ever produced. Human history has known more than its share
of fanatical, autocratic cultures, but whatever the religious or political excuses employed to justify their brutal actions, there tends
to come a time for these peoples when the battles have all been

fought and the riches have all been won, when the slow slide into hedonism and torpor begins—a decline that betrays the essential emptiness of the entire cultural project that preceded it. What differentiates the Mexica from the self-righteous empires that came before them and which continue to multiply so disturbingly in our own century, the quality that makes them more worthy of attention than the average group of murderous religious zealots, is the unwavering consistency with which they held to the vision that lay behind their outrageously destructive behavior.[4] Whatever else the Aztecs might have been, they were not spiritual hypocrites. The beliefs they professed in times of dire severity were adhered to as well in times of plenty, for those beliefs were oriented toward human desires far more mysterious and compelling than simple physical well-being.

Too little is known about the cultures of Teotihuacan and Tula, from whom the Aztecs borrowed most of their gods and most of their conceptions of the nature of the universe, to say whether they practiced human sacrifice simply as a method of placating the gods or whether they genuinely saw it as a method of releasing the human soul into a larger realm of spirit, but there is no question that for the Aztecs this was its most important function. The single greatest proof of this is that the act as practiced by the Mexica and their most enthusiastic neighbors was politically and economically far more damaging than helpful. Various theories have been advanced to explain the practice in "rational" terms, but none are convincing enough to account either for the volume of victims sacrificed in the course of a typical ceremonial year or for the brazenly flamboyant manner in which these sacrifices were carried out.

Many writers have stated matter-of-factly that sacrifice "supported the power of the state," but if we take the Aztecs at their word when they say that the state and the human beings it was composed of existed in order to ensure that the act of sacrifice would continue, this argument becomes somewhat circular. Evidence that the power of the Mexican state was more often than not hindered rather than helped by their devotion to the practice is particularly evident in the chronicles of its final years; in fact, it was one of the pivotal causes of their instantaneous collapse at the hands of the Spaniards. If the leaders of Tenochtitlan had not been so intent on keeping the fires of war burning in every direction, Cortez would not have had such an easy time finding Indian recruits to aid in his attack upon the city. By 1519 the Mexica's neighbors both distant and near were so fed up with life under them that they eagerly fell in with the Spaniards, only finding out later that they had eradicated one menace to their well-being only to have introduced an incalculably greater one. Even at the climax of the seven-month-long siege of Mexico (as the combined cities of Tenochtitlan and Tlatilulco came eventually to be called), when the Tenochca and Tlatilulca warriors were fighting constantly with little food or fresh water, they still found time to correctly sacrifice not only those Spaniards they succeeded in capturing but their horses as well, the heads of which they placed upon the city's skull racks along with those of their riders in honor of the gods who had at this point so completely deserted them.[5]

Several investigators, determined to find a commonsense motivation for sacrifice as practiced by the Aztecs, have gone so far as to suggest that since the flesh of most sacrificial victims was eaten, their entire preoccupation with it might have been motivated by nothing more than a shortage of protein in the Anahuac area. Such theories say more about their creators' inability to accept the reality of religious motivations as a force in human development than they do about the realities of the Aztec world, and are as far off the mark as the rationalizations of other writers that the Aztec people were inherently mean-spirited and cruel. Everything we know about the day-to-day realities of the Aztec cities suggests that life in them was ruled by a complex and ironic vision of the nature and meaning of human life whose dynamics cannot be reduced to any single, easily digestible cause, especially one that fails to address the intense psychological implications of the sacrificial act. If any remotely satisfactory explanation of why they did the things they did is to be found, one must turn to the spiritual world to which the Aztecs themselves looked for answers about their position and destiny in the universe.

The priests who transmitted the word of the gods to the rulers of the Aztec cities were in many ways the most powerful individuals in Aztec society. If anyone was reaping a secret profit from the actions of the state it should have been them, for the structure and the workings of that state had essentially been their invention. Next to the warrior and the heads of state—who almost without exception were either warriors or priests as well—these tormented figures enjoyed the highest prestige that Aztec society could give. Kings and princes consulted them on all matters, seeking advice on present events as well as those still to come, for like the shaman whose place in society he had partially taken over, the Aztec priest could see into the future. Yet his lofty station earned him no special privileges in the way of those worldly pleasures that for most of us make life worth living. He was celibate, and accustomed to grueling mortifications so severe that it was not uncommon for him to die from them. He awoke frequently during the night to tend to the needs of the gods, keeping braziers lit, intoning prayers, and indulging in a host of ritual demonstrations of piety usually involving a great deal of physical pain. In addition to lacerating his arms and legs, drawing ropes studded with maguey thorns through holes bored in his tongue or penis, and immersing himself in the chill waters of lakes and streams for extended periods of time, the Aztec priest traditionally smeared his entire body with a thick paste composed of blood, soot, tobacco, crushed scorpions, spiders, and rattlesnakes and a mixture of hallucinogenic plants and went wandering naked into the night, the stupefying mixture either lessening or increasing his natural terror of the nighttime landscape with its population of ghosts and demons.

The lot of the warrior with whom the priest shared top honors in Aztec society was not much better. Though he was allowed to make use of the comforts and conveniences that his predatory impositions on the goods and labors of others made possible and was treated with awe and veneration by the people of his own city, his enjoyment of these pleasures was always tempered by the knowledge that each new day could very easily be his last. Like the priest, the Aztec warrior did not pass through an initial testing period that if endured successfully gave way to a position of comparative ease. For both occupations, the testing period lasted as long as the office itself, and one cowardly action on the field of battle could immediately render null and void a decade of courageous ones. Just as the priest never ceased enduring penitential discomforts but strove instead to make himself continually more immune to them, the Aztec warrior, even if he attained to the highest offices obtainable, continued to take part in battles until very late in life. Though technically allowed to "retire" after reaching a certain age he very rarely had the chance to do so, for to reach old age in the Aztec cities was something of a miracle, especially if one was a career warrior who routinely risked his life year after year in skirmishes with rival cities. If, against all odds, such a warrior found himself intact after a lifetime of service to the state, he was by then so familiar with the presence of sudden death that his retirement years were tinged with a mood of bemused incredulity. Such survivors were treated with great respect, as were the elderly in general, and the crushing rules of state were relaxed for them. They could get drunk, for example, without suffering the death penalty that could be given to younger citizens caught inebriated. They had time to relax and ruminate on their past, which in itself was a great luxury in cities like Tenochtitlan where the fervor of statehood forced human life to proceed at the frenetic pace of some spartan summer camp where the chores never end and there are never enough badges to be won.

Preoccupation with warfare and the sacrificial drama even extended to the wealthy merchant class that grew up among these cities in their later years. Rich as they were, these individuals risked death almost as often as the warriors, for their profession took them frequently beyond the boundaries of their cities into faraway areas populated by peoples eager to express their hatred of the Aztecs. The constant ambushes they suffered in the field were one of the chief reasons this class was tolerated by the cities' rulers, for such actions furnished a convenient excuse for starting a war with whoever was responsible.

Such were the terms on which Mexico and its most enthusiastic neighbors allowed their citizens to take advantage of the worldly power they came to achieve in the latter decades of the fifteenth century. Whatever level of Aztec society is in question, one searches in vain for any individual who profited materially or emotionally from his or her way of life without having to endure some substantial catch. Their political and economic organizations were so structured that human happiness for its own sake was at best a secondary concern, for the gods had not created mortals to be happy. The job of mortals was to die in certain agreed-upon ways, which if properly brought off lent strength and meaning to the universe. The smaller human satisfactions were always seen in the light of the "nobly accomplished death" that justified the human form at the same time that it destroyed it. Because such a death, once achieved, was as irreversible as any other, there was no way for a living individual to know what the ideal state of the human person was like without achieving it—i.e., without dying—and this is what produced the atmosphere of gloom and doubt that pervaded life in the Aztec cities. That they had, in the truest sense of the term, no earthly reason to pursue these ideals so obsessively was acknowledged not only by the less war-obsessed peoples around them, who generally considered them crazy, but by the Aztecs themselves. Indeed, much of their arrogance was based not on their wealth and power but on their ability to make their own lives so consistently unpleasant in spite of their material advantages.

In the rites they practiced and in the myths they constructed about themselves, the Aztecs painted their universe as a harsh and supremely unsatisfactory place whose secret and diabolical workings they and only they had the fortitude and determination to face. While other less noble and serious-minded peoples might be content to take what pleasure they could from life while ignoring its more frightening implications, the Aztecs made sure that each of their cities' inhabitants were reminded of those implications every day of their lives. To paraphrase Bernal Díaz, everywhere the eyes of such a citizen turned they fell on death in one form or another; and just as a child born into a seafaring community may grow up to either hate or love the ocean but is seldom indifferent to it because its moods and movements determine the fabric of his or her entire life, so the individual of the Aztec cities might develop any number of strategies to cope with the fact of his or her mortality save one. Forgetfulness of death, even for a moment, was a luxury he or she was denied.

By whatever yardstick one chooses to measure them the Aztecs were an abnormally neurotic people. Their culture was visibly preoccupied with death as none before or after it has been, and for this reason it has been placed in a kind of quarantine by many students of ancient native cultures unable to see how it could positively contribute to an understanding of the profounder dimensions of the Indian worldview. But the Aztecs were not an anomaly in the centuries-long metropolitan tradition in Mesoamerica. In a sense they were that tradition's truest product, for the anxieties that the life of the city produced in them were indicative of the problems encountered by their predecessors who took the step from a wandering or village culture into a metropolitan one before them. Whether one chooses to talk of these problems in mythological, philosophical, or psychological terms, the damage they appear to have worked on the human spirit in Mesoamerica was expressed, over the centuries, in similar ways.[6]

Like those modern psychologists who have found the world of the psychotic to contain potentially beneficial insights into the shortcomings of everyday "healthy" states of human consciousness, the late Ernest Becker's investigations of the typical neurotic personality have revealed a similarly concealed wisdom of despair that contains significant parallels with the Aztecs' obsessive desire to berate the limitations of human existence—parallels that can help us frame that obsession in an interesting psychological perspective. In their insistence on dwelling morosely on the more puzzling and unpleasant aspects of life, the Aztecs behaved in a manner very similar to the neurotic of modern times who finds the "normal," "healthy" attitudes of his or her more well-adjusted fellows impossible to achieve. In his well-known book *The Denial of Death*, Becker examined the anxieties of such neurotics and put forth the suggestion that rather than suffering from a misunderstanding of the essential facts of human life these unfortunates suffer instead from a greater clarity of insight into them.

According to Becker, human beings are by nature unsatisfied with the constraints and vulnerabilities of the mortal condition and yearn for a dimly remembered state of grace beyond the frustrations of the mortal world and the extinction it inevitably leads to. Though he does not share our own admittedly romantic optimism about the possibility of a valid psychic existence beyond the body, Becker is convinced that a desire for this condition informs much or even all of human action and creates the secret obsession with physical mortality that he asserts is the trademark of the human condition. Becker's average, well-adjusted individual has effectively repressed this consuming frustration with mortality through a mass of denials and rationalizations, while the neurotic by comparison is forced to live without the protection of these denials. Burdened by a constant awareness of the overwhelming question of personal mortality, such an individual is incapable of seeing the day-to-day, flesh-and-blood world as anything but a ghostly and insubstantial land of phantoms, in which every living thing is perceived with paralyzing clarity to be moving toward extinction.

The following is a description of humanity's position in the universe from Becker's book. It is a description intended to address the modern, postreligious person but which, in its emphasis upon human vulnerability before the workings of a universe essentially indifferent to the individual's existence, comes very close to describing the pointless and carnivorous world of the Aztec cities:

> Man is reluctant to move out into the overwhelmingness of
> his world, the real dangers of it; he shrinks back from losing him-

self in the all-consuming appetites of others, from spinning out of control in the clutchings and clawings of men, beasts and machines. As an animal organism man senses the kind of planet he has been put down on, the nightmarish, demonic frenzy in which nature has unleashed billions of individual organismic appetites of all kinds—not to mention earthquakes, meteors, hurricanes, which seem to have their own hellish appetites. Each thing, in order to deliciously expand, is forever gobbling up others. Appetites may be innocent because they are naturally given, but any organism caught in the myriad cross-purposes of this planet is a potential victim of this very innocence—and it shrinks away from life lest it lose its own. Life can suck one up, sap his energies, submerge him, take away his self-control, give so much new experience so quickly that he will burst; make him stick out among others, emerge onto dangerous ground, load him up with new responsibilities which need great strength to bear, expose him to new contingencies, new chances. Above all there is the danger of a slip-up, an accident, a chance disease, and of course death, the final sucking-up, the total submergence and negation.[7]

Confronted with an experience of the universe described by this bleak and breathless but on one level quite accurate passage, the human psyche has two choices available to it. It can either retreat back into the various strategies of denial that Becker maintains most of us subconsciously rely on to avoid the unanswered questions about ultimate purpose and meaning that lie beneath the surface of daily reality, or it can move forward into a deepening awareness of the limitations of the human condition and the inevitability of death and personal extinction. According to the mystical tradition, this latter is the only true and beneficial direction that one can take. If pursued with an unflinching openness of mind, it will eventually lead to a point at which the disconnected, individual self-sense gives way to a larger dimension of reality in which the "I" that formerly experienced itself as cut off from the world is replaced by what could be called the "transcendent Self." This self perceives and experiences its unbreakable connection with an infinite dimension of spiritual forces very much like that perceived by the shaman when the physical world is suddenly rendered "transparent."

Becker and others have combined the insights of modern psychology with the descriptions of this state provided by ancient religious traditions to argue that the majority of human cultural productions, from artworks to empires, are grand but basically dishonest responses to a universally intuited problem with the shape and character of human life. In this view, human culture emerges as an ever-evolving set of strategies designed to avoid a direct confrontation with the physical body's inevitable disintegration through the use of symbolic, substitute forms of immortality. Wealth, power, and excessive carnality are the most common forms these strategies take, but numerous more devious ones exist as well, including pious devotion to religious systems that guarantee eternal afterlifes totally unrelated to the realities of authentic mystical experience, production of works of art whose greatness will assure that one's name is spoken long after one's body has faded away, and the reliance upon one's offspring to "continue the family name" as we found the head of One Hunahpu resorting to in the last chapter. While Becker is somewhat dubious about the extravagant claims of the mystical tradition, suspecting that the region of fabulous autonomy and undifferentiated bliss of which it speaks refers to nothing more than the paradise of early childhood when the infant enjoyed uninterrupted enfoldment in the warmth of the mother, others have taken these mystical assertions at their word, and the result, in books like Norman O. Brown's *Life Against Death* and Ken Wilber's *Up from Eden*, is an increasingly convincing picture of plain physical mortality as the leading character in humankind's secret history.[8]

From this perspective the Aztecs' preoccupation with death and their use of it to counteract the falsely consoling effects of an organized urban lifestyle takes on a surprising coherency. The esthetic sensitivity and cultural sophistication betrayed by the works of art and literature they have left behind hinted all along that there must have been more to the Aztecs' more repulsive religious rites than simple criminal sadism disguised as service to the gods. The problem was that the Aztecs themselves were of little help in uncovering the deeper motives that lay behind these rites, for like any good psychological subject they themselves were largely unaware of those deeper motivations. But once one grows somewhat used to their consistently offensive quality, those rites take on the quality of absurd burlesques, whose hidden purpose was to make the fragility of the human body overwhelmingly apparent in order that the expanded dimension of experience lying beyond the matrix of bodily concerns might be coaxed into manifestation once again.

A legend built around the Mexica's early expulsion from Culhuacan serves as a good preliminary example of the self-conscious nature of these rituals, and shows how the Mexica would come to use their reliance on them as a source of cultural pride. The story concerns a supernatural figure known as the Woman of Discord, yet another avatar of the many-mouthed Aztec Earth Mother whose hunger for human souls was one of the chief impetuses for continued war and sacrifice. It begins as the king of Culhuacan has assigned the beaten Mexica to the snake-filled shores of Tizapan. Huitzilopochtli, impatient as usual for the Mexica to establish their city, gives his dreaming priests the following instructions:

> We must have a woman who will be known as the woman of discord, to be worshipped as Our Grandmother when we have built our city. We must move away from this place, and we must show the world that we have bows and arrows, shields and swords. Prepare your weapons, then give Colhuacan [Bierhorst's spelling] a reason for war. Do this: go to their king and ask for his daughter to serve me as my priestess. He will give her to you, and she will become the woman of discord, as you will see.[9]

The Mexica go as instructed to request a daughter from the king, who complies after being told that she will be revered not only as a queen but as a goddess. Following Huitzilopochtli's further instructions, they then sacrifice the girl and invite the unsuspecting king to come and pay obeisance to his newly divinized daughter. The Mexica anxiously direct him to a darkened chamber, which he enters and dutifully begins laying out flowers and other ceremonial offerings. The king then lights some incense, and as the flames illuminate the interior of the room he sees before him one of the Mexican priests clad in his daughter's flayed skin. Fleeing in horror, he returns to Culhuacan and amasses his warriors, declaring that never before has he encountered a race of people so barbarous and disgusting.

The Mexica told this story about themselves, and the tone of this version shows the pride they took in their ability to disgust. Though the story itself is probably apocryphal, the practice of dressing up in the skin of flayed sacrificial victims was not. The Maya knew of it, as did the Toltecs, both of whom worshiped versions of a very ancient god that the Aztecs knew as Xipe Totec, "Our Lord the Flayed One." If not the first to practice the rite, the

Aztecs certainly took advantage of its potential to disturb with greater zest than had any of their predecessors—here as elsewhere making up in style for what they lacked in originality. On Xipe Totec's feast day in Tenochtitlan, the Dominican friar Fray Diego Durán reported,

> more men were slain than on any other because it was the most popular of all the solemnities. Even in the most wretched villages and in the wards of the towns men were sacrificed, to the point that the more I write and ask the more I am astonished to learn of so many rational human beings who died throughout the entire land each year, sacrificed to the devil.[10]

Next to his Franciscan predecessor Fray Bernardino de Sahagún, whose ten-volume *History of the Things of New Spain* is the most comprehensive and reliable source of information on Aztec life before the Conquest, Durán is perhaps the most trustworthy reporter on native customs: his description of this rite can be taken to be essentially accurate. The festivities begin with the sacrifice of the ixiptlas—human stand-ins—of several gods, including Quetzalcoatl, Tezcatlipoca, and Xipe Totec himself. Ixiptlas were an important part of most Aztec festivals, and from the moment one was chosen from the captive pool until the moment of his or her inevitable death, they were treated not so much as substitutes for the gods as actual incarnations of them. On this particular feast day, the ixiptlas were sacrificed and their hearts torn out "in the usual way," after which their bodies were flayed and their skins were each taken up by priests who

> donned the skins immediately and then took the names of the gods who had been impersonated. Over the skins they wore the garments and insignia of the same divinities, each man bearing the name of the god and considering himself divine. So it was that one faced the east, another the west, another the north, and still a fourth the south; and each one walked in that direction toward the people. Each of these had tied to him certain men as if they were his prisoners, thus showing his might. This ceremony was called Neteotoquiliztli, which means Impersonation of a God.[11]

These individuals, who wore the skins of the deceased ixiptlas in the traditional, reversed manner with what had formerly been the outside surface against the surface of their own bodies, were then bound to each other at the shins in order to suggest, according to Durán, the "unity and conformity" of the various gods they represented. This nightmarish assemblage then hobbled over to a nearby courtyard holding a temalacatl, a large and ornately carved variety of sacrificial stone with a long rope emerging from its center. Captive warriors were tied to this rope, on this and other occasions in the Aztec ceremonial year, and forced to engage in gladiatorial combat with four or more warriors from the home-city, who in addition to outnumbering him were substantially better armed. The captive warrior was given a wooden sword edged with feathers and encouraged to defend himself as best he could against the obsidian-edged swords of his attackers. This one-sided battle, which gave a captive warrior a final chance to demonstrate his bravery in the face of imminent death, was halted when one of the attacking four succeeded in striking a blow that visibly drew blood. Then, according to Durán, the attackers withdrew and the wounded but still-living victim was taken to another nearby stone and killed by heart sacrifice.

An accomplished warrior could delay his death for some time by keeping his attackers at bay with his feather-edged sword, and if really talented might even succeed in killing one of them. "This," says Durán, "occurred when the prisoner was a great man who had been a captain in the war in which he had been captured. Yet others were so fainthearted, so cowardly, that as soon as they were bound they lost all spirit, crouched, and allowed themselves to be wounded."[12]

Somewhere between thirty and fifty victims were sacrificed in this manner on the day in question, a process that took until nightfall to accomplish because of the longer time required to strike a valid blow upon the more plucky contestants. The whole process was watched over by the bound priests dressed in the skins and costumes of the previously slain ixiptlas. Later the priests removed the skins and presented them to another group of priests, who carefully washed them and hung them up on poles within a sacred enclosure. These skins played a further role the following day. Again according to Durán,

> very early the next day men would . . . borrow the skins in order to go begging. Poor people would do this in all the wards: borrow the skins, put them on, and over these wear the garments of the god Xipe. They then went about the city

and in each of the wards solicited alms from door to door. [The numbers of] these mendicants were twenty or twenty-five, depending upon the number of wards. They were not supposed to meet each other anywhere, in a home, on the street, or at crossroads, because if they encountered one another they were supposed to attack, assault, one another, fight until the skin and clothing had been torn. This was a statute, an ordinance of the temples. So the men avoided encountering one another, and because of this were accompanied by little boys who followed them. Others spied for them and carried the gifts which they had gathered.[13]

This procedure went on for forty consecutive days, at the conclusion of which the skins, now "black, abominable, nauseating, and ghastly to behold," were buried in the confines of the Temenos beneath Xipe Totec's temple.

Everyone in the land attended this burial, each man in his own temple; and when the ceremony had ended, a great sermon was pronounced by one of the dignitaries. This speech was filled with rhetoric and metaphors, delivered in the most elegant language. In this sermon the orator referred to our human misery, our low state, and to how much we owe to Him who created us. He advised everyone to live a quiet, peaceful life. He extolled fear, reverence, modesty, breeding, prudence, civility, submission and obedience, charity toward poor and wandering strangers. The preacher also condemned theft, fornication, adultery, the coveting of another's goods. At the end he extolled many virtues and condemned all evil, just as a Catholic preacher would moralize or preach, with all the fervor in the world.[14]

One can sympathize with the confusion suffered by Durán and the other well-intentioned churchmen who patiently recorded the details of such rites from the mouths of individuals who had taken part in them. What was one to make of a people whose language, architecture, and general demeanor was, in some respects at least, unarguably genteel, who in Durán's opinion loved their children as "no people on earth have loved their children," yet who sacrificed them almost as frequently as they did their adults? Durán's struggles with the wild inconsistencies of the Aztec character eventually led him to the conclusion that they comprised one of the Lost Tribes of Israel, who at some point in their wanderings out of their original homeland had fallen under the sway of the Devil. The

Aztecs, Durán thought, now depended on him and his fellow clergymen for their salvation. The many superficial similarities between Christian and Aztec iconography and ritual furthered his conviction in this matter, and in his writings he is frequently moved to remark on the cunning with which Satan had succeeded in mimicking the workings of the one true faith in these heathen rituals.

In our enlightened era of dispassionate observation, this explanation has yielded to the general consensus that the Aztecs were more or less blindly following the example of the peoples who had preceded them, using human sacrifice as a method of placating and currying favor with the gods of weather and vegetation on whom they depended for their continuing survival. This mundane and fairly straightforward variety of sacrifice has been practiced by various peoples throughout the course of history, and certainly the Aztecs practiced it with these ends in mind as well; but a powerfully effective religious act can involve many more levels of meaning than an observer or even an actual participant may realize, for the human imagination holds multiple dimensions that are at work even when one is not consciously aware of them. The Aztec priests and warriors who justified their bizarre practices by claiming that the gods demanded them were in fact performing those acts with another motive, unspoken yet more significant, in mind: by constantly submitting their own bodies and those of their fellows to elaborate and stylized destruction they were ensuring that the fact of mortality—and the potentially liberating spiritual ultimatums it led to—remained at the center of their attention at all times.

The life of the warrior was so structured that the possibility of death was never entirely out of his consciousness, and the life of the average citizen was only slightly less focused on that possibility through being witness to one, ten, or perhaps hundreds of such sacrifices in the courts and temples of the home city every day of the year. Following the schematas of human psychological response provided by the mystical traditions and their modern psychological interpreters, one can surmise that—for the more sensitive members of Aztec society at least—this perpetual bombardment of the psyche had two probable results. Either they broke down into a condition of total confusion and despair over the apparent cruelty and meaninglessness of their existence, or else this unrelenting confrontation with the question of death forced them to a point where they achieved a glimmering of the life beyond the body—a glimpse that begins as a spasm of absolute terror but which can then expand into a state of limitless bliss and power.

It was a common practice among monks of the Hindu and Buddhist traditions to loiter in the vicinity of burning grounds and cemeteries, and the injunction to meditate incessantly upon the fact of one's own mortality can be found in the literature of the world's other more sophisticated mystical traditions. The Tantric tradition is particularly rich in images of corpses, bones, and grinning skulls. While the Aztecs who created similar images never succeeded in creating a systematized doctrine explaining why such images were so dear to them, there is no reason to rule out the possibility that given the time they might not have arrived at one. As it happened, the Aztec confrontation with death and the state of spiritual integration that lay beyond it led to a partial and unformulated confrontation with the supermundane realities that lay beyond the purely physical realm, and the initial result was far more damaging than beneficial.

Spiritual traditions from shamanism to Zen Buddhism assert that a partial insight into deeper levels of reality can be far more damaging than no insight at all, for without proper guidance a neophyte can fall into states ranging from blank catatonia to grandiose delusions of limitless power. Modern psychologists who take the transpersonal dimension of human experience seriously have suggested that the yogi who professes union with the absolute ground of being and the psychotic who declares that he or she is God have both broken through into the same general dimension of experience, but whereas the former has done so in an integrated and coherent fashion, the latter has been taken into it unawares and is unprepared to meet the energies at work there. Though it certainly cannot be proved, it seems possible that certain individuals in Aztec society—the model warrior, who daily courted death and laughed at those incapable of the act, and the model priest, who flayed and hacked his way through numberless victims and carved up his own body as well—were acting under the sway of a similarly confused insight, the reality of which they aggressively celebrated, yet the implications of which they did not as yet fully comprehend.[15]

Aztec warriors, and those of the Mexica in particular, were notorious for placing themselves deliberately in situations where they were hopelessly outnumbered by their foes in order to demonstrate the authenticity of their indifference to death, and the Aztec priest who gouged and lacerated his tongue and penis beyond recognition made a similar point. The tongue is one of the most indispensable tools in allowing an individual to experience his or her own humanity and particularity: in addition to allowing one to enjoy food, it eases the sense of cosmic isolation through language; and this is especially the case in societies like that of the pre-Conquest Aztec, where the written word had not yet achieved the sophistication and nuance of the spoken. The penis—in its capacity as an avenue of union with the universe through the body of another—is so essential to human happiness that psychoanalysis has hinged its entire theory of human motivation upon the need to keep this organ intact. It does not take much effort to see that in mutilating this organ one is making a fairly profound and drastic statement about one's physicality.

Humans fear nothing so much as they fear separation, and by willfully breaking off these lines of physical and emotional interaction with the world outside the limitations of their flesh, these penitents were making a statement of far greater dimensions than the one they professed to be making. The priest who endured such mutilations was not expressing his devotion to the supernatural world so much as he was calling its very existence into question. By quite literally severing his ties with the physical realm, the mute and impotent priest encouraged the possibility of that complete and total breakdown of his psyche which everywhere in human spiritual history has been seen as the necessary prologue to transformatory insight. By willfully acting counter to every natural human impulse toward self-preservation and by irretrievably destroying the tools that allowed him to enjoy a modicum of human comfort and human joy, the Aztec priest was, in his own bizarre and misdirected way, following in the steps of both the shaman and the spiritual adept of distant mystical traditions. Both the shaman and the spiritual adept sought to recover their original, "angelic" identity by annihilating the twin forces of fear and desire that kept them prisoners of the conscripted, "fallen" world of physicality and death.

It was a quixotic and semi-articulated attempt to transcend the body's limitations—and it was far from successful—but it was powered by the same essential impulse that had empowered the shamanic traditions that had preceded it on the continent. Since the eclipse of those traditions and the drying up of the shamanic landscape they had admitted people into, the human body had become an increasingly vulnerable, increasingly problematic, and increasingly hopeless prison for the human soul. Like a cramped and leaky boat, adrift on a luminous and potentially annihilating sea from which it could no longer provide refuge, the human body was being aggressively left behind by these troubled spiritual adventurers in favor of a world beyond the body, whose characteristics they no longer had any real idea about but into which they were nevertheless increasingly willing to plunge.

Unless war, illness, or some other catastrophic misfortune forces such a confrontation upon them, most people in our own day get through their lives without ever being forced to a paralyzing confrontation with the indeterminacy of their existence. This experience is confined generally to neurotics, artists, and other varieties of the "oversensitive" character, who are treated today with more or less the same combination of condescension and awe that the shaman received from his or her more down-to-earth fellows in primitive times. Such individuals, more vulnerable than their fellows to the sensation of incompleteness that all human beings are born into but which most are capable of keeping largely out of their consciousness, are forced today to live in a world uniquely unequipped to help them in their struggle to find a viable solution to their dilemma. The mythological formulations that gave order and meaning to the universe in times past have been reduced to the status of mere curiosities, or at best have been refurbished and readapted to fit psychological systems. These systems, despite the best intentions, only cripple these formulations further by assigning the personages and entities they speak of to the "psyche," a vague and indeterminate region whose realities are never completely wedded to the "outside" realities of time, space, causality, and human mortality that are the true stopping blocks to individual human development. The various modern strategies of spiritual and psychological healing have much to learn from peoples like the Aztecs who put their money where their mouths were in terms of the encounter with mortality and physical limitation. Until those problems are faced head-on, the "spiritual experience" is only another cleverly devised method of avoiding all that is tragic and unanswerable in human existence.

In their more innovative moments, the Aztecs were a far more authentically engaged community of spiritual investigators than superficial appearances would suggest. Much of their persistent morbidity and violence was motivated by the same burning desire to transcend the limits of the human condition that has driven the world's greatest religious traditions. Mystics from many of those traditions have described the state of illumination, which propels one once and for all beyond the net of fear and desire in which the mind is normally trapped, as being preceded by a sensation of doubt so crushing and all-pervasive that many would-be illuminates are destroyed by it entirely. At this stage of its development the psyche tends to regard everything in the physical world with trepidation and loathing. Having seen without blinders to the heart of its limitations without yet having attained admittance to the saving expanses of the larger world that all along had lain beneath it, the individual finds him- or herself completely without refuge in the carnivorous, cold, and essentially meaningless universe described by Becker. In cultures supported by religious traditions that have come to recognize the characteristics of this difficult pass on the way to psychic completion, such people are provided with a supportive environment in which they may be allowed to fall to pieces—without influencing or being influenced by their community—until the point when, hopefully, their fragmented perceptions reunify in a larger manifold of consciousness. In shamanic communities, such people were sent off into the wilderness, whereas in more developed civilizations the solitude of the monastery or ashram served essentially the same function. But such was the unfamiliarity of the Aztecs with these potentially damaging and sometimes supremely energizing mental states that no effective system existed to safeguard against the deluded and misdirected actions that individuals in their grip could be susceptible to.

It may seem unrealistic to suggest that, even provided that this state of temporary imbalance exists as a regularly occurring phenomenon of human psychological experience, it would be capable of manifesting on such a large scale that the worldview this state encourages could take over an entire civilization. But civilizations have their moods as much as individuals do: a country or a people can stagnate for centuries and suddenly cohere into an explosive period of transformation under the leadership of one or many individuals. Renaissance Italy and Hitler's Germany are two particularly vivid examples of the contrasting directions such movements can take, and the unbelievable achievements and the unity of temperament demonstrated by the Aztec peoples in the centuries of their rise to power were distinctive enough to suggest that they too, for whatever reasons, were in the grip of a similar compulsion.

The Aztecs were a confused and contradictory people: their conceptions of the universe were as numerous and incompatible as were the borrowed or hastily formulated gods who moved about within it, yet their world did possess one quality that consistently informed each of its multiple and fragmented parts and supplied as close an approximation of ultimate meaning as they were able to formulate at the difficult station of spiritual development they found themselves in. This quality was anxiety, and the god who came closest to achieving a position of absolute rulership over their universe did so because that was the quality he most stood for. This highest of all the Aztec gods, who in Burr Cartwright Brundage's words "was the final statement with which they glossed the universe,"[16] was Tezcatlipoca, the ancient confounder of the Toltecs and the being responsible for everything unpredictable and frustrating about human life in general.

In the several volumes that he has devoted to Aztec history and thought, Brundage spends much time trying to penetrate to the heart of Tezcatlipoca's character, and arrives at the conclusion that he achieved the status he did in Aztec belief because he represented more completely than any other god the potentially demonic nature of the universe. Tezcatlipoca ruled over the fate of the individual, but unlike most "primitive" gods of human fate and fortune he was largely immune to the pleas and promises of the mortals whose life and happiness depended on him. It was thanks to Tezcatlipoca that people could rise to positions of wealth and influence, and it was thanks to him as well that sudden, unforeseeable disaster robbed them of such positions overnight. Praying to him for assistance might produce positive results but could just as easily provoke further wrath, for though allpowerful he was completely devoid of compassion or pity for his hapless human subjects.

The Aztecs had what we would term "slaves," but in keeping with their ever unpredictable character treated these individuals with more respect and compassion than their ritual habits would lead one to suspect. Slave status could be achieved through illegal actions, offensive behavior, or plain laziness, but whatever the circumstances, this status could always be reversed through diligent effort. Tezcatlipoca was considered to be particularly partial to slaves because, as the lowest members of human society, they embodied the essential powerlessness of all people, who, whatever their position in the petty hierarchies of mortals, were equally vulnerable to the sudden, unpredictable blows of accident or illness with which he loved to surprise his subjects. A number of days in the Aztec calendar were devoted to Tezcatlipoca, and on one of these all slaves were traditionally excused from their labors and presented with gifts by their masters, thereby acknowledging their essential equality in the eyes of the uncaring gods.

Life in the Aztec cities was precarious and unsettling enough without the added burden of a god whose main activity was tricking individuals into a false sense of security only to abruptly pull the rug out from under their feet, yet this was the chief activity of Tezcatlipoca in those cities, just as it had apparently been in the city of Tula. In Tenochtitlan, the atmosphere of dread and foreboding the presence of this god produced was further heightened by the year-round presence of an ixiptla of the god, who wandered and danced at night through the city's streets and avenues covered in a suit of jingling bells and playing a reed flute. Like other ixiptlas, this poetically conceived figure was chosen from the general pool of captive warriors waiting for their time of sacrifice. Special care was taken in selecting Tezcatlipoca's ixiptla: the winning candidate ideally was young and flawlessly handsome, for the god that he was to "become" for a year possessed the Dionysian ability to manifest in attractive as well as monstrous guises. (Priests out wandering the nighttime roads covered in the hallucinatory insect-snake paste mentioned above were more likely to encounter him in the latter form. To them he could appear as a shrouded, groaning corpse or as the ghastly "Broken Face," an avatar of the god who, according to Brundage, "hopped along darkened roads on a single taloned foot.").[17]

The young man chosen to represent the god in human form could look forward to a year of honors and attentions outstripping those received by all but the highest ranking rulers. Reaction to being selected for the honor probably varied from individual to individual, depending on the level of personal investment in the Aztec way of life each had managed to achieve. Evidence that some ixiptlas were less eager than others to take on the mingled glories and drawbacks of the role is suggested by the fact that they were accompanied at all times by "a retinue of eight young male companions as well as four veteran warriors who," says Brundage, "acted as guards; they attended him day and night both to amuse him and to prevent his escape."[18] Like the other positions of highest honor in Aztec society, that of the ixiptla was heavily and intentionally ambiguous. The perpetual catch-22 of the Aztec religious endeavor—that human life only had meaning when it approximated to the divine, but approximating to the divine always entailed physical death—held for this figure as much as it did for the warrior or the priest.

While the ixiptla was considered to be the god him- or herself, the figure who played the god did not partake in the condition of possession commonly achieved in more primitive, shamanism-oriented communities. Shamans typically are capable of mimicking the movements and the voices of various gods and spirits in their trance states, but they keep this up for relatively short periods of time. The Aztec ixiptla probably did not achieve this kind of psychological transformation. Brundage feels that the ixiptla provided a "clear visual packet" that "satisfied the curiosity and expectations" of the Aztec worshipers about the gods they spent so much of their time serving.[19] Yet this playacting apparently did not succeed in creating a significantly greater degree of intimacy or understanding between mortal and god, for the individual who filled the god's shoes did so only in a superficial manner. Ultimately the ixiptla's charisma and power depended upon the fact that he or she was to die, for after the shaman's ecstatic methods had been lost, death was the only method available to the religious practitioner of genuinely leaving the human realm behind. Damaging as this obsession with the death of the spiritual practitioner was, both to all those who had to die to achieve spiritual "legitimacy" and to those they left behind, it was the last effective gesture left to them.

Flawed as it was, the drama of the ixiptla was nonetheless a powerful one. Like much of Aztec cult, it substituted flash for substance in its attempt to reattain to the verities of the spiritual domain that have served to give meaning to human life in every age. Tezcatlipoca's ixiptla was given the grandest treatment of all in deference to his status as the god of contradiction, and in the final days of his tenure the Aztecs' preoccupation with the ironies of human existence, where pain and pleasure, beauty and horror, intermingle in maddeningly inexplicable ways, came to the fore.

"Came the month of his celebration," says Brundage, "and the public veneration accorded to him rose to peaks unusual even for the Aztecs." The representative of the god was now presented with four concubines with whom he was supposed to indulge in the "sexual acrobatics for which the god was famous."

> Five days before the *ixiptla* was to meet his end, the ruler of Tenochtitlan ceremoniously acknowledged the god's sovereignty by divesting himself of his insignia of rule and turning it over to him. After that the ruler retired incommunicado within his palace, thus delivering the city over to its legitimate lord Tezcatlipoca. During these last days the *ixiptla*, accompanied by his women, danced and sang and was banqueted at various places in the city.
>
> In a splendid finale, the *ixiptla*, accompanied by his four wives, was then taken in a state canoe from Tenochtitlan to the south shore of Lake Tezcoco. Once they were all disembarked, his wives left him and he moved on, surrounded by escorts, priests, and other participants, to a very ancient shrine of his at a place called Tlapitzahuayan. Here he slowly ascended the fronting staircase while ostentatiously breaking the flutes upon which he had played during the year. On reaching the summit he was swiftly dispatched and his opened body . . . contrary to custom—was not tumbled down the steps but was instead reverently carried. At the bottom the body was decapitated and dismembered, and that night his flesh was served up in a solemn collation to all the great lords of Mexico. On this occasion the newly chosen *ixiptla* . . . also partook of the flesh, thus highlighting the uninterrupted presence of the god.[20]

The peoples of the Aztec cities flanking Lake Tezcoco, as well as the fanatical core of Mexica at its center, were not so divorced from normal human sensitivity that they failed to see the perverse humor and what we would call the shock value in rites like this. It was largely these qualities that made the rites interesting to them. In a world of dreams the most horrible event can turn out to be the best, for its shocks the dreamer awake, out of the shadow world in which he or she had been trapped without knowing it. Modern "existential" psychologists like Becker echo the warnings of numerous mystical traditions when they suggest that for a human being caught in the web of bodily concerns, bodily fears, and bodily desires no longer fed by a larger ground of meaning beyond it, life can become an opaque and seemingly gratuitous affair—a cave of illusions such as is described in Plato's famous allegory. In a culture such as ours, where the words "spirit" and "soul" no longer carry much resonance and the blinding realities of the "other world behind this one" remain no more than speculative possibilities, an individual hungry for an authentic experience of those realities can end up seeking them in largely negative ways, just as the Aztec priest and warrior did.[21]

▲▲▲▲▲▲▲
▼▼▼▼▼▼▼

The Aztecs identified with the sun more strongly than with any other of the celestial bodies that moved across the skies above them and through the devouring regions beneath. Several conflicting scenarios were developed to explain its origins and the significance of its movements, all of which grew out of the original shamanic scenario of initiatory descent and rebirth but which were modified in various ways to better address the Aztecs' specifically bleak and desperate view of life. One such myth that they held particularly close to their hearts asserted that the sun was originally a very different entity than the one that passed over their heads each day. This being was known as Nanahuatl, which translates roughly into "Diseased One," and in this myth of his transformation there occurs a moment that, taken in itself, is emblematic of the Aztecs' entire situation in the universe. According to this story the sun was born at the beginning of the present era when the gods, conferring in darkness at the ruins of Teotihuacan, decided that one of their number needed to sacrifice himself in order to become the sun of the fifth and final epoch. A fire was built and straws were drawn to see which god should throw himself into the transformatory flames, and the loser was Nanahuatl. This pathetic creature, whose body was covered with sores and who, according to the myth, was so unpleasant to look at that the other gods could fix their eyes on him only with difficulty, was dusted all over with white chalk and pasted with downy feathers in the manner traditional for sacrificial victims and directed to leap into the flames.

This myth was created by a people for whom immolation was not a theoretical matter. Human victims were cast into flames on several occasions during the Aztec ceremonial year, and a listener would have had no difficulty sympathizing with Nanahuatl at this point, for he had seen this method of transformation practiced and knew that it was not pleasant. Nanahuatl hemmed and hawed for some moments and then, summoning all his resolve, rushed toward the flames and vanished into them.

Following along the lines of the story of Quetzalcoatl Topiltzin's immolation, one version of the story relates that "after his body had completely burned he descended to the Dead Land and traveled underground until he reached the earth's edge on the east."[22] Here, at the threshold between the underworld of initiatory fire and the blue sky of day, the Diseased One suddenly hesitates, for his transformation from a sickly and insignificant creature into a luminous celestial power has rendered him imperious and arrogant. Hovering just beneath the surface of the earth, he proclaims to the waiting gods that he will move no further up into the heavens until each one of them has submitted to sacrifice as well. Xolotl, an unpleasant underworld avatar of Quetzalcoatl's, whose name translates as "Dog," "Monster," or "Penis," does the honors, sacrificing all the gods and then himself in order that the new sun will consent to rise and the fifth and final epoch of the universe can begin.

This was one of many myths used by the Aztecs to justify to themselves their penchant for human sacrifice. On its most superficial level it makes the now familiar point that the sun cannot move without human hearts, and that it is the job of mortals in the fifth epoch of the universe to provide him with them. This explanation is fine as far as it goes but does not account for some of the story's more peculiar details. Why, for example, is Nanahuatl weak and diseased before he undergoes his transformation, and why is he haughty and distant once he has achieved it? The answer is that in addition to providing a model for the mechanics of the universe, this myth served to provide the individual of Aztec times—particularly the warrior—with an allegory of his own position in the cosmos. Like Nanahuatl before he marshals himself for the rush into the fires of pain and potential extinction, the Aztec considered himself "diseased" by the stamp of human mortality. Like Nanahuatl he was unsure of what might await him beyond the perimeters of physical existence, for no figure existed in his society to show the way into and back out of the superphysical dimension, those secrets having been temporarily lost with the breakdown of the shamanic traditions. Poised uncertainly at the edge of a larger world whose existence they intuited but with which they had lost all authentic means of contact, the Aztec warrior and the Aztec priest played tentatively at the boundaries of the mortal condition. They flirted daily with personal extinction and, watching as their fellows slid past them into the abyss of death, grew ever more fearful of the condition that would await them there when their own time came.

As the years of Aztec domination passed, this grueling and apparently unresolvable confrontation with the realities hiding beyond the veil of the physical world began to wear at the stamina of these cities' rulers, priests, and warriors. The customs and practices they borrowed from the peoples who came before them, as well as those they invented themselves, so dramatically pointed out the tenuous nature of human life and the ultimate vanity of human endeavor that ultimately they managed to bring the entire cultural project into question. Despite their tremendous arrogance, the Aztecs had always suspected that their re-creation of Toltec civilization suffered from a crucial flaw—a misunderstanding about the workings of the universe and the actions it demanded of them—that angered the gods and in time would provoke the return of the vanished priest-king Quetzalcoatl from his place of exile in the eastern sea. In the decades immediately preceding Cortez's arrival, the suspicion was growing among the Aztecs that the time of their cities was approaching its end, that the tangible productions of rock and mortar they had designed to court the attentions of the spirit world had only served to alienate them completely, and that if a solution to their dilemma was not found soon the results would be disastrous.

Tenochtitlan was the last great pyramidal city to be built in Mesoamerica, and as such was the last statement of a two-thousand-year architectural and cultural tradition that had attempted to approximate the dimensions of the supernatural world and link them convincingly to the doings of humanity. Like its predecessors, the Aztec pyramid was both a stage and a cosmic landmark: a self-proclaimed vortex of spiritual energy through which humans passed from this world to the next as thousands watched from below. But also like its predecessors, the passageway it claimed to open up turned out to be only a one-way street to the realms beyond the physical dimension, and the sacrificial drama it supported ended by betraying the ideal of mutual communication between the world of the flesh and the world of the spirit it had been designed to open up.

It is often pointed out by those writers who consider them to be second-rate Indians that the workmanship of Aztec temples is inferior in design and detail to those of their Maya predecessors. But considering that unlike the Maya, who intended their productions to last for all eternity, the Aztecs suspected that their pyramids and temples might turn out to be no more than momentary follies that could at any time be wiped from the face of the earth by the offended gods, the fact that they were built at all is remarkable. The world's first cities were eternal cities, or at least were considered to be so by the peoples who designed them. Sumer, Athens, Rome, Tikal, and Bonampak were not built with obsolescence in mind, but Tenochtitlan was, for its architects suffered from the bleak but insightful suspicion that worldly empires were somehow beside the point and would never bring to their makers the longed-for experience of divinity.

No single individual embodied Aztec civilization's frustrations with itself and its resulting penchant for self-sabotage more completely than the pre-Conquest Mexica's last and most famous ruler, Montezuma II. Montezuma came to power in 1503, sixteen years before the first boatloads of Spaniards anchored off the eastern coast near what is now Veracruz. Mexico at that time was at the height of its power and its unpopularity, and seemed by outward appearances to be destined to continue in this growth for some time to come. This steady advance began to visibly lose momentum the moment Montezuma assumed the mat of rulership—a mat that according to legend he and all who came before him were ordained to guard until the day when the banished god of the Feathered Serpent would return to assume it. The nagging sensation that their empire had thus far betrayed entirely that trust seems to have crystallized in Montezuma the moment he was instated, for this position put him directly under the gaze of the resentful gods of the land—particularly Quetzalcoatl. He responded to the burden of guilt and fear imposed by this position in eccentric but typically Aztec fashion.

Montezuma was, like all of the Mexican rulers before him, a successful initiate in the cult of warfare, having proved himself appropriately contemptuous of death many times on the field of battle. Yet his years as ruler were characterized by acts of cowardice and self-sabotage very uncharacteristic of an Aztec king. Under the pretext of an unswerving devotion to maintaining the "purity" of the Mexican state, Montezuma succeeded very early on in alienating himself from his own people by instating needlessly severe limitations on the rights of commoners, banning them from positions of service in his palace, and ordering that any non-noble who looked directly at him when he walked the streets of Tenochtitlan be executed on the spot. These insulting gestures were followed by others toward the rulers of Mexico's sister cities in the Triple Alliance, with whom continuing good relations were crucial if Tenochtitlan was to avoid being crushed by its surrounding subject-kingdoms.

Oddly enough, Montezuma's belief that Quetzalcoatl was to return in the time of his rule was not just a flourish made up by native chroniclers after the Conquest but a genuine conviction that grew with each year he remained in office. As the fateful year of 1519, or One Reed, grew closer, Montezuma's fears are said to have been fueled by a series of omens, presaging his people's fall, that grew ever more numerous and ever more sinister. Buildings and temples in Tenochtitlan caught fire spontaneously, the waters of the lake boiled, and a strange bird was brought in from the marshes by hunters—a creature with a mirror on its head such as the sorcerer Tezcatlipoca had shown to Quetzalcoatl in the days preceding his departure from Tula. Though most of these presages of the disaster to come were invented after the Conquest, a few may have been based on actual occurrences. Among the most curious of these is the ball of flame that appeared in the skies over Anahuac in 1509. Though no astronomical explanation has been found for it, the consistency of the various sources describing this phenomenon suggests that a celestial body, appearing after darkness had fallen and continuing into the morning hours night after night for over a year, was indeed witnessed by the fearful inhabitants of Tenochtitlan and the other cities of the lake.

Montezuma monitored this and the other anomalies with ever increasing dread, consulting soothsayers, magicians, and priests on their meaning and having these individuals executed whenever they predicted the doom-laden future that he himself increasingly suspected. By the time the first reports of floating islands carrying bearded, manlike creatures who rode about on giant dogs and carried sticks that spat fire reached Tenochtitlan, Montezuma was already well on the way to nervous collapse. Weeks later when these creatures arrived at the shores of Lake Tezcoco they were able to ride, with an enormous entourage of the Mexica's Indian enemies behind them, right across one of the city's three causeways and into the center of Tenochtitlan without resistance. There they found the Mexica's king awaiting them, ready to hand over to the gods the mantle of rulership that mortals had once again failed so miserably to fulfill.

Brundage's interpretations of Aztec thought are considered risqué by academic standards, but he avoids for the most part the kind of highly speculative psychologizing we are indulging in here. With Montezuma, however, he cannot resist taking more than his usual amount of liberties, and it is interesting that his attempt at unraveling that king's character concludes with a passage that might have come from Becker:

> The anxiety that lies in all of us and is our common heritage as men was in Montezuma expressed with a singular vividness. His fear of death was pronounced and resulted at the end of his life in the abject surrender of all his outward dignity. His suspicions of himself and fear of failure forced him into the extreme policies and the typical assertiveness of the self-righteous man. He demanded to be treated almost as a god, more so, it would appear, than had been the case with previous Mexica rulers. His pride was gross and indeed abnormal.[23]

This combination of arrogance and self-doubt, this desire to attain to the condition of a god while at the same time fearing the wrath of the true gods of the cosmos at such presumption, lay at the center not only of Montezuma's character but of his entire civilization's as well. Like the sickly god that had transformed himself into the sun that lit their epoch, this last king had vacillated between the desire to avoid death and the desire to run at full speed into the mystery that lay beyond it, and when at last the "true gods" arrived in his earthly city, he gave it back to them with the shame of that vacillation showing plainly in his actions.[24]

One of the greatest ironies of the Aztec collapse is that the chief mistake these peoples and their predecessors had made in creating their cities—mistaking a corporeal symbol of the spirit for the spirit itself—was made one final time in their dealings with Cortez. The major problem with the Aztec metropolises—and with those of the civilizations that came before them—was that they functioned as substitute paradises: superimpositions upon the authentic landscape of spirit into which they were supposed to have provided an entrance. The larger their cities grew, the harder it became for them to keep the realities of the spirit world in focus, so that when fate presented them with an ersatz Quetzalcoatl in the form of Cortez they were so hopelessly out of touch with authentic manifestations of the divine that they failed to see him for the imposter he was until it was too late.

Though Cortez had quickly acquainted himself with enough of Nahua mythology to exploit this case of mistaken identity to maximum advantage, his assertions that he was in fact the god Quetzalcoatl were rapidly seen through by Tenochtitlan's less credulous citizens. Only Montezuma, whether out of fear or genuine conviction, continued to assert that the Spaniards were gods and not merely oddly dressed humans, and by the time of his death—he was surreptitiously killed by the Spaniards when he had ceased to be of use to them—he had become the subject of mingled hate and embarrassment among the people he had so completely failed. The last long burst of Mexican resistance to Spain was orchestrated by Cuauhtemoc, Montezuma's nephew who was sworn into power after it was realized that Montezuma himself had become a worthless mouthpiece of the invaders.

Many myths were constructed around the decline of Montezuma, most of which do not attempt to paint him in the kinder light of hindsight but describe him as the same ruthless and cowardly figure that appears in the more historical sources. These myths are interesting, however, in the reasons they give for this cowardice: his real sin is not toward the people he let down but toward the gods of the supernatural world, who see him as a hypocrite caught up in the delusions of material power and thus as a traitor to the spiritual heritage that his people were meant to live up to.

One story[25] tells us that Montezuma "loved nothing more than to order great monuments that would make him famous," thereby placing petty human pride before authentic commerce with the world of spirit. All the fabulous constructions of his artisans were greeted with the presumptuous complaint that they were "not splendid enough for Mexico," the tone of the story suggesting that he really meant that they were not splendid enough for him.

Deciding that the enormous, round stone on which prisoners were sacrificed to Huitzilopochtli was not sufficiently imposing, Montezuma in this story sends his stonecutters off into the countryside to find a rock from which to cut a larger one. One is found and cut roughly to shape where it lies, the finished product being satisfactorily larger than its predecessor. Laborers then begin the long process of hauling it back to Tenochtitlan, in the course of which the stone suddenly comes to a halt, snapping the ropes that bind it. As more are being attached the stone utters ominously, "Try what you will."

> Suddenly the shouting stopped. "Why do you pull me?" said the stone. "I am not about to turn over and go, I am not to be pulled where you want me to go."
> Quietly the men kept working. "Then pull me," it said. "I'll talk to you later." And with that the stone slid forward, traveling easily as far as Tlapitzahuayan. There the haulers decided to rest for the day, while two stonecutters went ahead to warn Montezuma that the great stone had begun to talk.
> "Are you drunk?" said the king when they gave him the news. "Why come here telling me lies?" Then he called for his storekeeper and had the two messengers locked up.

Refusing to believe what is obviously a bad omen, Montezuma nevertheless sends a group of lords out to examine the stone, which continues to protest on the grounds that Montezuma has "tried to make himself greater than our lord who created the sky and the earth. But pull me if you must, you poor ones. Let's go."

Halting intermittently to forecast doom, the stone is eventually dragged halfway across one of the three causeways leading over the lake into Tenochtitlan. As Montezuma waits on the other side with flowers and sacrificial victims to appease the recalcitrant stone, it once more comes to a halt, this time with the words " 'here and no farther.' And although the causeway was made of cedar beams seven hands thick, the stone broke through them, crashing into the water with a noise like thunder. All the men who were tied to the ropes were dragged down and killed, and many others were wounded."

Based on an actual event in which a number of laborers were killed when a new and larger sacrificial stone that Montezuma had in fact ordered broke through a causeway and dragged them spiraling down with it, this story with its reference to "our lord who created the sky and the earth" is certainly tainted by Christian influence. After the Conquest, Aztec mythmakers were more or less obligated to include such references in the tales they told to the

Spanish friars, and most of the mythological material we possess from this period contains occasional lip service to the new religion. The "moral" of this story is, however, entirely native. Like the rulers of the civilizations that came before him, Montezuma suffers here from a confusion of worldly and divine power that makes him think he is a god when he is really only a dangerously presumptuous mortal. This is a common enough form of hubris for a king to suffer from, but its implications here are deeper than the stated moral—that mortals should not behave like gods, for the real gods will become annoyed and punish them—suggests. The stone is speaking on behalf of the same pre-Christian landscape that sent the sorcerer Tezcatlipoca to Tula centuries before, and once again its anger at the "poor ones" of the human community results from their failure to meet and trade with its energies in an honest or effective fashion. Read with the vanished shamanic perspective in mind—a perspective that the Aztec worldview grew out of and to which it still was effectively related despite its urban and military leanings—the real meaning of the stone's actions might be interpreted as follows: "Do not behave like a god in a misdirected way; do not try to substitute human power for divine power, for the two are not the same and the attempt will leave you alone with your human power, which, great as it may be, you will soon find to be worthless."

The point to be gained from tales like this one is not that human beings should be content as menials to the supernatural world, for in the most integrated primitive communities this is never the case. Cooperation and collaboration, both physical and spiritual, are the benchmarks of such communities, and it is these qualities that the Mesoamerican metropolises consistently failed to achieve. Through their essentially earnest efforts at creating a physical arena for the play of those larger energies that demand expression if human life is to be more than an interminable struggle for brute physical survival, the Aztecs and their predecessors produced cities that again and again walled them off from those energies completely, and the result was always disaster. Time after time, these cities end up affronting the "true gods" of heaven and earth—gods whose images may vary in accordance with geography and human temperament but who throughout human history have possessed one enduring quality by which they may be identified: they make the lives of those who revere them authentically meaningful. If proof of this be needed, it can be found in the inexplicable contentment of peoples like the Huichols, who despite the rudeness of their dwellings and their general lack of worldly finery have remained as a whole an infinitely more adjusted group than any of Mesoamerica's rich but tormented cities.

Another tale told of Montezuma's decline makes this point in more direct fashion using the same imagery of the "magical flight" that Eliade discovered to be such a universal theme among both shamanic and postshamanic cultures. The hero of this story, a poor farmer, is working in his fields when he is abruptly swept up into the sky by an enormous bird such as carried away many a fledgling initiate in Siberia and the Americas in the days when shamanism was at its height. This bird takes the farmer to a mountain in the sky that corresponds to the world-center—the *axis mundi* that connects the levels of the cosmos and of which the Mesoamerican pyramid has already been seen to be a reproduction—and into a cave where an entity called the "lord of all power" is awaiting him. The lord beckons him into a "dazzling chamber" where he is surprised to find the body of his king, Montezuma, lying unconscious. The farmer is presented with a handful of flowers and a burning tube filled with tobacco—a kind of Aztec cigarette—and told to

> look carefully at this miserable one who feels nothing. He is so drunk with pride that he closes his eyes to the whole world, and if you want to know how far it has carried him, hold your lighted smoking tube against his thigh and you will see that he doesn't feel it.[26]

The farmer hesitates in fear for a moment, then does as told. "You see," says the voice when the body of the king gives no reaction, "how drunk he is with his own power. It is for this reason that I brought you here."

The farmer is then whisked back down to earth by the enormous bird with instructions to go to the palace of his king and tell him what he has witnessed. Summoning all his courage, the farmer goes to Tenochtitlan and gains an audience with Montezuma. When he relates the details of his dream flight, the king, already plagued with omens of his imminent decline, flies into a characteristic rage and orders the man locked up and left to starve. After the innocent farmer is dragged away, Montezuma in terror examines his thigh, for the outlandish tale has reminded him of a dream he had the night before, in which he had imagined that he slept in a mountain in the sky and that a man had burned him there with a smoking tube. Sure enough he finds there a wound, which suddenly begins to pain him beyond endurance. "For four days he lay suffering," the story concludes, "and only with great difficulty were his doctors able to make him well."

Through the details and the incidental symbolism of this story, the true nature of Montezuma's crimes and the real identity of the beings he has offended overrule any Christian-style morals that the clerics who took it down might hopefully have tried to attribute to it. The "world" that Montezuma's arrogance has blinded him to is the spirit world, and the numbed body that the farmer finds within the world-mountain is the ruler's *nagual*, his dream body, which, like that of One Hunahpu's, has become impotent and incapable of action within the world of supernatural force that underlies the physical world and upon which it depends for nourishment. The "sin" of Montezuma was allowing that essential side of himself to wither away from neglect, for unlike his shamanic predecessors who strove tirelessly to recover that original vision that penetrated to the ends of the earth, he had chosen in the end to be seduced by the mundane satisfactions of worldly wealth and power. By the time he and, by association, the Aztecs in general had realized the extent of their failure it was too late, for the weight of their material cities had once again shut them off from all access to the spirit realm except through the irrevocable action of sacrifice.

In a final hint at the tale's true meaning, its author or authors state that the king was sick for four days after discovering the wound—a reference to the eight-day journey taken by Venus through the earth before its rebirth in the east. Unlike his mentor Quetzalcoatl after he threw himself into the flames on the border of the eastern sea, Montezuma is "sick"—that is, dead—for only half of the eight-day initiatory journey undertaken by the human soul when it leaves the frame of the body. Thus he is destined, like One Hunahpu before him, to vanish at the nadir of the universe on the tree of death, whose roots are those of extinction but whose branches flower in the world above this one with the promise of a life beyond the fears, desires, and misdirected longings of the hazardous middle-world of human life and human struggle.

4

The Benevolent Apocalypse

▼▼

All of you undisturbed cities,
haven't you ever longed for the Enemy?
Rainer Maria Rilke

THE CONQUEST of Mexico-Tenochtitlan was one of the grisliest episodes in the centuries-long string of atrocities that make up the story of the "settling" of the American continent. The number of people killed in the course of the Conquest was unprecedented, and shocked even the Aztecs. More shocking still were the reasons for all this carnage—reasons that the Aztecs soon identified as the accumulation of gold for the greater glory of a distant god who, despite his apparent greatness, did not seem as fascinating and venerable to his proclaimed servants as gold itself, which the Spaniards were seen to worship as a kind of concretized divinity.

Though the Spaniards spoke confidently and insistently of their relationship with Jesucristo, who ruled from a pleasant-enough sounding paradise (which like Quetzalcoatl's Tlapallan was located either in the heavens above or somewhere to the east), even the Aztecs—a people famous for their open-mindedness toward foreign gods—had trouble taking what the invaders had to say seriously.[1] To begin with, the Spaniards had demonstrated from the very beginning of their relations with the Indians that they were great liars, and as they acted with such consistent dishonesty in other matters there was no reason to think they would act any differently when it came to describing their gods. Their constant talk of compassion and heavenly charity was strongly in contrast to their actual behavior toward their new Indian subjects, whom they made a habit of raping, torturing, and otherwise humiliating long after the last flames of the siege of Tenochtitlan had died out. The Indians soon discovered that the friars who followed in the wake of the Conquistadors to commence the huge task of converting the New World were often less hypocritical and prone to brutality than their fellows, but there was not much in the incomprehensible and comparatively bland religious ceremonies offered by these figures that was of interest to native sensibility. Dancing, song, and the religious theatrics at which the Aztecs excelled were condemned as the work of the Devil, and despite the Spaniards' propensity to murder indiscriminately when gold or other riches were at stake, the taking of life in a religious context was inexplicably condemned.

Yet in Mexico-Tenochtitlan as elsewhere on the continent, native gods and conceptions refused to be stamped out overnight, creeping back after an interval into the lives of the reluctantly Christianized Indians, who continued to think about and speak with those divinities as they had done for centuries past, though now in hushed tones and behind closed doors. The Aztecs came under European influence at a time in their history when their relationship with the divine world was terrifically strained, and despite its apparent inadequacies they looked toward the new religion for hints at a way of resolving the numerous contradictions that continued to inform their religious life in the years following the Conquest.

The most impressive evidence of this continued attempt to achieve a fruitful dialogue with the gods is contained in the ninety-one song-chapters of the *Cantares Mexicanos*. This document—the largest single repository of Nahuatl "poetry"—has only very recently been given a definitive English translation by John Bierhorst, whose versions of Aztec myths we have been using throughout this book. Bierhorst is not only the first to translate the *Cantares* in their entirety, but also the first to provide a viable interpretation of their meaning. The language of these songs is elegant but extremely cryptic, for they were incanted, Bierhorst believes, only by elite groups of initiates in a clandestine cult that flourished in and around Tenochtitlan in the middle decades of the sixteenth century that used them as part of a ritual designed to conjure up the spirits of dead warriors and heroes from the Aztec past.

Recitation of these songs under the proper conditions (about which we know almost nothing because of the pains taken by the participants to hide them from the meddling Spaniards) achieved more than a simple recounting of past events and personages—it brought them to life. The Ghost Song Ritual, as Bierhorst has termed it, most probably involved dancing and singing to the point of ecstatic transport, in which the participant either witnessed the descent of spirit warriors into the precincts of the ritual dancing-ground or was himself swept out of it into the midst of a land beyond, whose characteristics are described in the *Cantares* in fascinating detail. As it is presented in these texts, this land is similar or perhaps identical to the warriors' Paradise that sacrificial victims were thought to ascend into in pre-Conquest ideology, with the important difference that in the *Cantares* it is described from the inside. The longed-for reciprocity between the living and the dead—the essential intermingling of human and spiritual realities through convincing trance experience that so evaded the Aztecs in the time of their worldly dominance—seems here to have been at least partially granted to them. The Aztecs were a people in love with catastrophe: destruction in whatever form was a sign that ultimate truths were afoot, and whether they were the agents of that destruction or its victims, they were capable of finding significance and the promise of great things where others would find only fear and despair. If their world in the years before the Conquest had been materially rich but haunted by a sense of spiritual impoverishment, their post-Conquest world was one in which those riches had been exposed as the illusory comforts the Aztecs had always suspected them to have been. Human purpose and human meaning were now fragmented and confused almost beyond all recall, and out of this grim situation some of the most talented of their remaining poets and thinkers found the impetus to explode in a last, visionary burst of spiritual affirmation.

As grand and vivid as the situations narrated in these secret rituals were, outsiders witnessing one of them would most likely not have been awed so much as puzzled by what they saw. The circular dancing, drumming, and repetitive singing they are thought to have featured are integral to the vision-inducing ceremonies of other native peoples—and the hallucinogenic drugs that played an important part in some of those ceremonies may also have found their way into the *Cantares* rituals. As the ritual intensity generated by the drums, dancing, and the shared focus of attention of the participants reached a certain pitch, a hypothetical outside observer might have witnessed one, then several, then many dancers shifting over into the distinctive valence of those possessed by ecstatic states of consciousness. Perhaps their dancing would increase in energy at this point; perhaps they would stare wildly before them at a descending world of lights and forces that the outside observer would be unable to make out; or perhaps instead their bodies would slump to the ground, remaining there as their spirits traveled far away, to regions of such strangeness that they would need to be visited again and again and thought about for a long time before they could begin to be fully understood.

Scenarios like this might very well have taken place, but this is largely a matter of conjecture. The details of such rituals had by necessity to remain secret, and the secret was well kept. The only solid surviving hint of what a *Cantares*-style ritual might have looked like comes from a popular native dance known as the "volador," an elaborate and probably quite ancient performance practiced here and there in Mesoamerica to this day. The center of the volador performance is an upright pole with a swiveling platform on the top large enough to accommodate several dancers dressed up in feathered costumes that those familiar with the specifics of Aztec cult would immediately identify with sacrificial candidates. Bierhorst describes the essentials of this dance as follows:

> Ropes wound around the pole pass through grooves in the platform and are tied to the dancers' bodies. On signal they fling themselves backward and into the air, and the platform begins to rotate. As the ropes unwind, the dancers come whirling downward in continually widening circles until they reach the ground. In some cases they hang upside down and spread their arms.[2]

Popular at the time of the Conquest, this oddly literal enactment of the spirit-warrior's return to earth along the axis of the flowering world tree was one of the ways in which the Aztec ritualist managed to express his penchant for public dramatizations of spiritual events even after the Conquest had robbed him of his old power and authority. Though no longer allowed to rip out human hearts and dance around in flayed skins, the Aztecs could occasionally perform more subdued rites like this one without interference because the Spaniards mistakenly took them to be no more than simple carnival amusements and benign displays of native acrobatic skills. In time, this is in fact what they became, and when such elaborate dances are performed today in Mexico it is doubtful that much, if any, of their original significance survives in the hearts of those who repeat them. In Mexico in the decades immediately after the Conquest such was not the case, and it must have given a secret satisfaction to those still versed in the old customs to see such a dance being performed right out in the open, before the eyes of the uncomprehending invaders.

10. *A whimsical European rendition of the Volador dance.*

The version of this dance practiced by the *Cantares* ritualists—which entailed fits of authentic ecstasy and other manifestations of genuine religious engagement to which the Spaniards would not have taken kindly—did not take place in public, and as a result we are left to guess at the specifics of its presentation. If the *Cantares* authors did indeed go to the trouble of constructing such elaborate stage props for their own more blatantly subversive, ecstatic renditions of the volador dance, it was certainly not in order to vent their acrobatic skills. From the evidence of the *Cantares* texts, the visible movements of the dance were but the outward manifestations of a profound spiritual drama in which the descending, feathered dancers betrayed their original connection not only to the cult of war, but to the ancient shamanic practices in which the image of a man clothed all in feathers had first received its most potent significations.

The landscape most often visited by the ecstatic *Cantares* participant is described in the texts as a pulsing, otherworldly realm of lights and colors different from, yet in many ways more real than the world of ordinary daylight. Its glorious vistas must have been a welcome relief from the frustrations of sixteenth-century colonial Mexico, and as with similar landscapes discovered elsewhere in post-Conquest America in reaction to European suppression of native life and native realities, its contours and denizens are described in heartfelt and ironic contrast to the absurdities of life under European rule. Like those other mass migrations into spiritual regions beyond the reach of the white intruders (the best known of which is the Ghost Dance Religion that sprang up among the Sioux and other western tribes in the late 1800s), the *Cantares* rituals were partly reactionary in nature. The desire for former times, hatred of whites and the cruel and idiotic way of life they engendered, clandestine dreams of being rescued by cosmic forces that burn up or sweep the hateful invaders back to where they came from—these themes occur in the *Cantares* just as they do in the scores of "nativist" religions that grew up throughout the Americas as a response to the European presence. These movements did not cease after the first ones were crushed or sputtered out, but kept on cropping up among one or another disaffected native people well into this century. Though they vary widely in terms of their sophistication and the specifics of the "new world" era they inevitably predict is about to dawn, these movements possess a remarkable consistency of form—a consistency due not so much to the Christian themes and motifs that they frequently borrow, nor to the circumstances of white suppression that initiated them, but to the surprising uniformity of American Indian mythological thought.

Indians throughout the Americas tended to conceive of time as unfolding in a series of ages or creations—a belief that for many was intimately tied to a parallel conception that physical existence, as men and women know it, had been derived originally from spiritual sources and was destined to return to those sources when the drama of incarnate reality had thoroughly played itself out. Whatever stage of this progressive unfolding a people saw themselves as living in, the disastrous white presence usually convinced them that its end was at hand and that an entirely new era of existence was about to be ushered in. The impossibility of life under the whites—a people who behaved in aggressively nonsensical fashion but who also possessed impossible devices indicating that an age of miracles was once again at hand—tended to convince the subjugated Indian peoples that the ordered world of meaning in which they had lived, with its regular seasons of animal and vegetable growth and decay, was winding down, to be replaced by the topsy-turvy conditions that prevail in the chaotic period between cosmic ages (the "time between the times," as it is sometimes called). When world ages grind to a stop, meanings become unhinged: natural and social hierarchies break down and people, plants, and animals behave in ways contrary to their usual habits. Nothing makes sense anymore because the veil of ordered coherency that had shielded mortal creatures from the uncanny and potentially destructive forces of divinity has been torn loose. The world-supporting gods—the Bacabs of Maya lore and their many equivalents in other tribal mythologies—abandon their task of holding up the sky and the heavens flood down upon the worldly plain. The dead return to life, rising out of the ground like shoots of corn or flooding down out of the heavens above.

The ambiguous nature of the coming apocalypse was a cause for much speculation in pre-Conquest America, but whether it was regarded with fear or anticipation, or a combination of the two, the concept was of tremendous importance in giving sense to the present universe and accounting for its more troublesome aspects—particularly that homesickness for a half-remembered state of grace with which the Indian thinker was so often preoccupied. Throughout the Americas, reaction to the promised return of the gods varied considerably from one people to another, largely depending on the health of each people's relationship with the forces of the supernatural in their present state of partial occultation. The Huichols, who spoke daily to the gods and ancestral spirits and visited their country bodily on a regular, yearly basis, looked forward to the return of that domain more or less without reservation. The Aztecs by comparison, in keeping with their tradition of mingled desire for and fear of the supernatural world, alternately courted the end of the present world epoch and held elaborate rituals to ward it off.[3]

The Aztecs were by no means the only native people to identify the white invaders with returning supernatural forces. Some groups conceived of the whites as the gods themselves, while others saw them as a relatively insignificant, preliminary manifestation of the apocalypse—buffoonlike creatures whom the gods had sent down to alert the "true" people that the time of apocalyptic transition to new modes of being was at hand. The Aztecs, particularly the Tenochtitlan Mexica responsible for most of the songs in the *Cantares Mexicanos*, had begun with the first assumption—that the Spaniards were the gods themselves—but quickly moved on to the second. This realization of the essential irrelevance of the white invaders and the catastrophe they had wrought produced a number of problems. After the first few decades of life under them, there was no longer much argument among the Aztecs that, although the predicted destruction of their empire had indeed occurred as many had expected, the holocaust had only been a partial one. The greatest city in Anahuac had been demolished and rebuilt, the stones of its pyramids and sacrificial temples now refashioned into the churches, banks, and prisons of the new rulers. But outside, beyond the limits of the city, the natural world continued as it always had, oblivious to the absurd station to which Mexico, the aspirant center of the universe and the axis of its multileveled regions, had been reduced. The true apocalypse, which the Aztecs had been awaiting with a combination of longing and dread and which would have brought the too-well-known rhythms of black night and ordinary daylight to a joyous or nightmarish close, had failed to arrive. Likewise the true gods who were supposed to return when the mortar of the world weakened had failed to emerge as well, leaving the beaten Aztecs alone in their ruined city with their odious, mortal conquerors.

Such were the conditions in which the *Cantares Mexicanos* were written: conditions at once tragic and deeply anticlimactic, in which the opaque, the mundane, and the distinctly unmagical realities of the everyday world with its painful and pointless struggles and conflicts appeared to have triumphed once and for all. Obsessed as they were with endings, the Aztecs had imagined many for their own civilization, some triumphant but most disastrous and even nightmarish, but never one so ignominious as the one being forced upon them now—an end deprived of all drama, honor, and divine significance, as humiliating to the gods as it was to them. In addition to suffering a complete and catastrophic military defeat, the Aztecs were forced to watch in disbelief as the Spaniards calmly entered into their most holy and restricted temples without any harm being done to them by the gods in whose honor they had been built. After rooting around in these intensely sacred confines in search of gold trinkets, the Spaniards calmly set about dismantling them, all without a hint of protest from the gods who in the times before the Conquest would have wiped humanity from the face of the earth for such transgressions.

Heroically, and once again against overwhelming odds, the post-Conquest Mexica set about fighting their final battle—a battle that, unlike those physical ones that preceded it, was waged in secret by a few instead of many and entailed no spilling of blood. Because the Spanish Conquest both fulfilled and contradicted the tenets of Aztec religion, destroying the cultural and intellectual complex of Aztec civilization but leaving the lugubrious, exterior world of daily toil and tedium intact, the Aztecs felt compelled to somehow complete the destruction initiated by the Spaniards through spiritual means. The most positive aspect of the worldly apocalypse as it is described in scores of American Indian mythic speculations is that it brings mundane time—the time of work and death and human ignorance—to an end, replacing it with a paradisal state in which these inconveniences are left behind. In the post-Conquest world of the Aztecs, as for other Indians laboring under white pressure, it was just these unattractive aspects that the apocalypse had failed to remove, and this drove the Indian thinker to the hopeful conclusion that the real apocalypse still lay somewhere in the future, awaiting appropriate actions on their part to manifest itself. Using the patchwork assembly of religious tenets they had been uneasily struggling to galvanize into a coherent way of life at the time of their collapse, the Mexica created a ritual environment that they hoped would initiate the final movement in the drama of incarnate life.

The luminous tree- and flower-filled expanses of the magical region visited by the *Cantares* ritualists are showered by crystalline rains and swept over by radiant, fluttering birds—birds that on closer inspection turn out to be the spirits of slain warriors enjoying their promised reward of an eternal afterlife. This uncanny and supremely attractive region goes by many names in the *Cantares*: "God's home, the place of tassel plumes," the "House of Paintings" or "House of Colors," "spirit land," "land of flowers," and others that similarly emphasize its qualities of beauty and hallucinatory abundance. In dense, highly metaphorical language, the songs again and again describe a similar course of events: longing to establish contact with this fabulous world, a singer will entreat the kings and princes of vanished times to appear again before him on the dancing-ground. If he delivers his song with sufficient feeling and skill, his efforts will transform the darkened square in which he sings into a blossoming, heavenly battlefield— the paradisal landscape brought to earth—into which a flood of ghost-warriors descend to sing, dance, and do battle. Ghosts from rival cities descend as well, and historic battles are reenacted. Here as in actual Aztec warfare, the actions of singing, dancing, and fighting are strangely intermingled. The Aztec conception of war as a kind of ultraserious dance and the old theme of battle as a method of ecstatic transport reach new heights of lyric expression in these passages, and to the same essential ends: as more and more ghost-warriors are "killed," more come flooding out of the heavens to take their place until the demarcation between heaven and earth, life and death, is blotted out of recognition by the rush of souls passing back and forth across it.

Here is a typical passage describing a rush of ghost-warriors descending to earth in answer to a successful song evocation:

> They're scattering down on us, sprinkling down on us: they're combat
> flowers, giving pleasure to the Only Spirit, God the father.
> Shields, com-
> panions, are shrilling. Let them stand upon this flood.
> There! The blaze is seething, stirring. Honor is won, shield fame
> is won.

Lords are strewn at the place of bells.
They'll never tire, these war flowers. They're massing ah! at the
    flood's
  edge. These jaguar flowers, these shield flowers, are
      blossoming. Lords
  are strewn at the place of bells. (XXIV)[4]

Though these songs tend to begin on a note of indeterminacy and despair—usually with the singer lamenting his isolation on the broken earth that stretches grimly about him in all directions—they do not hold this tone for long. As the singer sends words up into the empty skies, the heavens, up to now so deaf to Aztec humanity's plight and their pleas for aid or answers, suddenly and miraculously begin to condense above the singer and rain down upon him and his comrades. This "rain" or "flood" is not of water but of discrete entities—"songs," "flowers," or brightly colored birds, which Bierhorst argues are the souls of dead warriors, returning at last to transform the face of the earth through their electrifying presence. At this point in the ritual's unfolding, a second, significant turn in the proceedings occurs: as ghost-warriors descend in response to the invocations of the singer, mortals rise into Paradise to take their place, the rule of the game being that a spirit of the dead can reenter the earthly plain only when a participant in the ritual travels up from earth to take his place in Paradise. Though the reasons for this rule are never explained, it is entirely consistent with Aztec beliefs about the physical and spiritual dimensions. Like a vial containing two chemically incompatible liquids, one clear and one opaque, which blend when shaken furiously but separate as soon as the vial is stilled, human life and the world of the spirit refuse to be reconciled for more than an instant in the *Cantares*—an instant that in pre-Conquest days occurred when the sacrificial knife descended with, in the words of a Spanish commentator, "all the quickness in the world,"[5] to break open the human frame and release the imprisoned spirit-essence in the form of the human heart.

Back and forth go the participants, the living and the dead, dancing, singing, fighting, and in general shaking up the oppressive solidity of the material world that the false apocalypse of the Spanish Conquest had so infuriatingly failed to disturb. In these songs, if not before them, the hidden, affirmative quality of warfare and

sacrificial destruction is completely revealed. War is now fully described as what it had always implicitly been for the Aztecs: a
dance enacted to reunite the disaffected levels of the universe. The
storming of mundane realities by the forces of the supermundane
world described in these songs addressed and attempted to overcome the same essential ambiguities of life on earth and beyond it
that warfare itself had. Bierhorst notes in the introduction to his
translation that in the conception of battle used by these songs,
"the desirability of victory must be weighed against the desirability
of death on the battlefield. Sometimes it almost appears as though
the enemy enjoys the happier outcome."[6] The paradoxical affection between "enemies," the mingled fear and desire for the realms
beyond death, and the constant approximations toward grace and
weightlessness demonstrated by the physical participants—all
these themes are present in these spiritualized versions of battle
just as they had been in the real thing. The difference is that in the
case of the *Cantares* ritual, the reunion between the living and the
dead and the mutually estranged worlds of spirit and flesh they
represent has come one step closer to being actually accomplished.
"Most songs," Bierhorst continues, "do not allude to any specific
battle. In these schematized compositions the singer produces
ghosts of his own tribe or allied tribes, seemingly for the purpose
of creating a state of bliss on earth."[7] For an instant, the dead and
the living stand side by side, and in this brief flash of interpenetration, the mending of the cosmic axis, which humanity, the gods,
and all of creation had so long been awaiting, is achieved.

Thus beyond simple, retroactive victories over their various enemies, be they Spanish or Indian, these ritual re-creations of battle
and the flesh-and-blood versions they based themselves on, concealed beneath their more petty motivations the promise of an
apocalyptic confusion of realities, the desired result of which was
not victory over a physical enemy but over the stultifying opacity
of the fallen, purely physical world. As with battle as the Aztecs
had practiced it in the days of their dominion, so now with this
entirely spiritualized form of warfare, it was the strangely liberating process of battle itself, and not the material ends it achieved,
that was of significance. The only truly consequential victory
achieved by warfare—the one that drove the Aztecs to practice it
in such an apparently gratuitous manner in their days of glory and
which drove them now to reformulate its postulates and attitudes
in a strictly ritualized framework—was that of the human soul

over the ties of physical embodiment. In both versions of the game the enemy is a co-conspirator against the tyranny of that embodiment and the enfeebling web of concerns and desires it creates. The act of killing or being killed is equal if done in proper form, for it sends a soul across the barrier separating the known from the unknown and in so doing further undermines that barrier to glorious effect.

However incongruous the Christian/Indian crosscurrents that make up the *Cantares* ritual, through it that astonishingly ancient and widespread dream of the soul's feathery autonomy—which had been pursued in ancient America and elsewhere long before the advent of Christianity and its own familiar winged embodiments of the life beyond the body—was realized one last time in Mexico in potent, essentially native terms. The paradisal landscape that these songs and the ritualized dances that are believed to have accompanied them conjured up was less a simple, two-dimensional borrowing from Christianity than a renewed vision of Tlapallan, at the center of which rose not a cross but a perennially blooming tree, amidst the quetzal-colored foliage of which the souls of warriors initiated into eternity were gathered, waiting to descend to earth.

Though unified by their essential purpose of accomplishing an apocalyptic reunion of the physical and spiritual dimensions, the *Cantares* are not unanimous in the conclusions they draw about the nature and feasibility of that union. They were the work of a number of authors with strongly differing opinions on an essentially shared group of themes, and the *Cantares* ritual was used by them not only as a method of ecstatic transport but as a forum for argument. Beneath their arcane language, the questions posed and argued in them are familiar ones: Is there an afterlife, or does human life end with the body? If there is an afterlife, what are its characteristics? Is it divided into a heavenly and a hellish region? If so, what does one need to do to enter into the heavenly one? Are war and human sacrifice an entryway or a barrier to the other world? And so on. This open-minded and pragmatic quality is what gives the *Cantares* their charm and originality as well as their power. As with all productions of the genuinely religious mind, they speak with the urgency and authority that come from a strongly felt desire for transformative knowledge—a need for the real at whatever cost—and that sense of urgency compensates for their many inconsistencies and contradictions.

> Can this earth be home? We're / living in a place of poverty and torment. Where can I go get corn? / Where can I go look for it? Will I resow it like a flower? Will I replant it? / Will my father, will my mother, be an ear of milk corn, a baby ear of / corn, on earth? For this I weep: no one has regard for people: they've left / us in bereavement here on earth, where the road to Mictlan lies, the / place of going down, the place where all are shorn. Do we really live / again in the Place Unknown? Can our hearts have faith? In a coffer, in a / wickerwork, Life Giver hides us: he shrouds us. Will I see my mother, / my father? Will I look at their faces? Will they give me what I seek: their / songs, their words? For this I weep: no one has regard for people: they've / left us in the place of bereavement here on earth. (XVIII)

In the eyes of the authors of songs like this one, heaven and hell and the lost roads that led into and out of these regions were as much of a mystery now as they had ever been before. The meager compensations that the physical world had offered to take the Aztecs' minds off the terrors or wonders that waited beyond had now fallen away, leaving these survivors of the Conquest completely alone with their doubts. Those doubts are voiced with persistent regularity amidst the more assured descriptions of the warriors' Paradise. In the above passage the promise of the visionary Paradise is overshadowed by fears of Mictlan, the Aztec underworld, whose unseen presence continued to threaten Aztec hopes for a fruitful life beyond the body after the dubious comforts of their visible, worldly empire had been destroyed. Elsewhere it is earthly life itself that is brought into abrupt and unflattering comparison with the realm of light and color, just as it had been in pre-Conquest times, but now with an increased sense of irony at the distance that separated the miseries of the material world from the unspeakable fulfillments of Paradise:

> As a parrot, as a swan, I fly along on earth. My heart is wine-
>   drunk.

I'm a quetzal, arriving in the Only Spirit's place of rain,
     beautifully singing
   above the flowers. I utter songs, and my hearts rejoice.
A flower flood foams over the earth: my hearts are wine-drunk.
Pitiable, I grieve, earth is no one's home. (XLVI)

Joy and ambiguity, longing for the world beyond the physical and apprehension at its potentially annihilating capacities, alternate in the *Cantares,* as does the authors' belief in the traditional methods of attaining it—methods now severely brought into question by the collapse of the Aztec cosmos. Having been told by their new masters that theirs was a false religion and that sacrificial practice would bar them from the true, Christian Paradise, the authors again and again weigh Christian and Aztec conceptions against each other in an attempt to arrive at the correct attitude to strike toward the vertiginous spaces of the intuited world of spirit that lies behind the flawed physical world as its summation and its final justification.[8] This open-minded consideration of religious alternatives makes for strange conjunctions of native and Christian motifs and characters: in the fragment from song XXIV quoted above for example, "the Only Spirit, God the father" is dragged into a description of supernatural warfare in which he would not seem to have much place. Elsewhere, Jesucristo himself enters in full Aztec war garb ready for battle, and in one amusing sequence the pope is described shooting darts at the Aztecs with a jade blowgun from his throne in Castile. Such references tend to put off readers who think that once touched by Christian influence Indian thought is irremediably cheapened and no longer worth investigation. Such is not the case with the best of the *Cantares* however, for the spirit of authentic metaphysical inquiry with which they were composed, and the visionary experiences attained by their most talented participants, were strong enough to reenergize the tired Christian symbolism forced upon them by their conquerors and bring it to life in a new and unexpected context.

Much more lies in the balance in these songs than the choice of one "official" creed over another, for to the Aztecs a religion could still potentially function as a hands-on strategy for entrance into worlds of meaning and experience that give answers to the tragedies and contradictions of the material realm. One of these songs' most persistent laments—that worldly goods and worldly fame are no more than transient illusions and that the march of human history is a blind parade toward an ignoble extinction in the depths of Mictlan—has prompted modern interpreters to attempt comparisons between their worldview and that of twentieth-century existentialism. "Nothing we say here is real," bemoans the singer of one song frequently quoted by authors attempting the existentialist comparison: "What we say on earth is only a dream, as if we stood sleeping. We really utter it to no one" (XVIII). The follies of the material productions of pyramid and palace are condemned elsewhere with phrases like "No one returns in stone, no one returns in wood" (LXXXIII) and in this impressively gloomy passage:

> It would seem that no one's home is earth.
>   No one can remain. Plumes splinter, painting ruin, flowers
>   wither. All
>   are headed for His home.
> Such is life. People get to know each other briefly here on earth
>   near you
>   and in your presence, Life Giver. No one can remain. Plumes
>   splinter,
>   paintings ruin, flowers wither. All are headed for His home.
>   (LXXXII)

Bierhorst quite rightly warns against such tempting comparisons, for despite the familiar note these passages may seem to sound, they continue to treat human life in relation to a region of indisputably greater realities from out of which it has fallen and to which it keenly desires to return. Though the *Cantares* speak of the possible meaninglessness of the human condition, most do so within the context of another, larger world of divine significances from which, in some of their myths, the Aztecs speculated that even the gods themselves had been driven at the time of the world's creation.[9]

The reality of this spiritual dimension is taken largely for granted in the *Cantares:* even the more morose of these songs are consistently directed toward a living god who, be it Christian, Aztec, or a combination formed from these two traditions, has no place in those modern schools of thought that style themselves as postreligious. A concept such as the death of God (or Life Giver, as this Aztec-Christian hybrid is often called in the songs) would have made no sense to the Aztec thinkers who produced these pieces, for the reality they most often call into question is not that of divinity but of the human soul, and it is that entity's potential connections with the lost, luminous ground of divine realities that are the cause of all the alternating jubilation, despair, and feverish speculations that fill these songs. In spite of their frequent lapses into doubt and confusion over their relationship to the worlds of meaning above and beneath that plain of earth that now more than ever was "no one's home," in most of the *Cantares* this empty dread is finally overwhelmed by an act of directed imagination that invokes the transforming presence of "paradise" and the odd, warlike angels who inhabit it.[10]

> Let people see, let people marvel in a house of colors. Let God
>   Life Giver's
>   creations be here.
> By making us aware of his creations, God Life Giver torments
>   us, causes
>   us to crave his garden of song flowers.
> Already in a springtime, in a springtime, we are walking here,
>   upon this
>   field. A green-swan downpour roars upon us in Water Plain.
> Lightning strikes from the four directions. Golden flowers are
>   reviving.
>   There, the Mexican princes are alive. (XIV)

Before Bierhorst's reinterpretation, passages like this one made little or no sense, and were generally ignored by translators and interpreters in favor of those with a more easily apprehensible, "philosophical" content unencumbered by embarrassing references to gods and disembodied spirits. The powerful, somewhat surreal sense of the last lines of this passage is lost if it is not understood that the "golden flowers" refer to palpable entities, and that the word "there" in the last line points to a spiritual manifestation taking place not in the past or in some distant hell or heaven, but right before the speaker's eyes. These sudden, jolting appearances are common in the *Cantares*, and appear to be a source of great joy to those who describe them. The consistent enthusiasm with which these appearances are greeted is important for understanding the place and significance of these songs in the drama of the Aztec religious quest, for it bears a strong similarity to that sense of buoyancy and release that the spectacle of human sacrifice gave to its practitioners in the days before the Spaniards brought it to a halt.

As different as these two phenomena—sacrificial death and induced hallucination—might seem to be, their essential effect on the initiates who experienced them was probably quite similar. The forceful destruction of a human body and the potent visualization of a spiritual presence, be it radiant and angelic or merely spooky and unsettling, are both methods of assault on the limitations of human perception, the difference being that in each case the assault comes from different sides of the barrier separating spiritual from mundane realities. In the last chapter we suggested that the death of a warrior on the sacrificial block degraded the solidity of the material world, for when presented with the fact of death the Aztec mind found it incomprehensible that something as vital and knowable as the human personality could simply vanish into nothingness. The perception of a spiritual entity such as the returning "flowers" described in the *Cantares* is a partial answer to the question raised by such a death: it answers it "from the other side" as it were, and furthers belief in what had been suspected by the Aztecs all along—that reality as humans perceive it in the course of their day-to-day waking consciousness is but a fraction of the cosmic totality.[11]

Not content to leave behind the questions of human life and transhuman meaning that had dogged them in their days of rule, the Aztecs developed the *Cantares* ritual to aid them in concluding the essential search for a new method of spiritual practice that would allow them to experience while alive the reality of dimensions beyond the physical. The breaking open of body after body in pre-Conquest times had functioned as a first approximation of another, deeper act of destruction that the ritualists of the *Cantares* continued to furtively experiment with in spite of all the pressures forcing them away from such preoccupations. The "argument" of the *Cantares*—as best it can be extricated from the mass of confusing, contradictory, and occasionally silly points of view expressed in them—is this: human experience is composed of two fundamentally separate yet related dimensions—the life "here on earth," as the *Cantares* would say, and the life "there beyond." Relations between these two dimensions are, at the present point of cosmic evolution, in a state of uncomfortable alienation from each other, but if human life is to have any ultimate significance this state of alienation must be overcome, even if this entails the complete destruction of the physical world itself.

The soul's vehicle in the course of its time on earth is the human body, and in pre-Conquest time that vehicle had been subjected to an unending series of stylized attacks in the blind hope that this breaking would free another, hidden agency of potency: the soul, or magical body. In the *Cantares* ritual, that same unquenchable desire for a proof of the life beyond the body emerges, amid a mass of syncretistic confusions, to provide a strangely fitting epilogue to the brief but furious Aztec religious endeavor. In those scattered passages that describe the timeless and colorful intensities of the spirit world flooding down upon the broken, parched, and exhausted world of post-Conquest Tenochtitlan, we are given an indisputably authentic taste of the paradisal vision that has driven all of the great mystical traditions—a vision that ultimately had been the impetus for many of the heinous actions of the Aztec state that had come before.

The Aztecs are a difficult people to like or understand, and it would be facile to excuse all of the misery they caused themselves and others on the grounds of the hidden core of authentic spiritual aspiration that informed them at their best and deepest moments. Yet that a people as contorted and ruthless as they can be found to have been at all concerned with such matters is ultimately a very positive discovery. In our own post-Freudian age, where for many it has become a habit to think of the deeper human motivations as little more than base and unsubtle appetites, it is encouraging to be able to discover, in a people as outwardly nasty as the Aztecs, a set of concealed impulses directed not by fear and lust but rather by beauty, transcendence, and spiritual autonomy.

The same wild promise of the human soul's place of origin in a region beyond the ambiguities of the present human condition has been left to us by other ancient civilizations in much less ambiguous terms than those used by the Aztecs, and this promise perhaps should not be outgrown with the mythologically-minded ways of life that first gave voice to it.[12] The refastening of human and transhuman realities that gave us the word "religion" has been described and attempted in countless ways over the past few thousand years, and if the language used to describe it often sounds foolish to us, the project itself should not. The task of making the multiple worlds one continues to present itself in our own day and age, and the various transpersonal psychologies currently struggling to map out that project in modern terms might take consolation from the fact that even a people as seemingly distanced from charity, compassion, and balanced understanding as the Aztecs can themselves be found to have been seeking those and other lost, essential qualities, in a land that begins where the tangible world ends and where the souls of mortals appear as quetzal-colored birds.

With the *Cantares* we come to the end of Aztec religion proper, and to the end of our account as well. This book has tried to frame a few moments in the long and still only dimly understood history of Mesoamerican religion in the context of a search, and stories of searches cry out, at their conclusions, for solutions and ultimate discoveries—for fabulous treasures that render all the strife and confusion that had come before worthwhile. In the days before the Maya were discovered to be the fathers of warfare in Mesoamerica, such treasures were fairly easy to come by. Whether as the brilliant survivors of sunken continents like Atlantis or Lumeria or as intergallactic emissaries zapped down to earth by a supercosmic intelligence anxious to instruct earthlings in the dangers of atomic war and air pollution, the ancient Mesoamericans of popular imagination were always capable of providing readers of greater-than-average credulity with the qualities they most wanted in a lost civilization. What is interesting about such accounts is that the commodity they delivered, at the expense of most of the known archaeological and ethnographic facts, is very similar to what the ancient Mesoamericans themselves were searching for in their own mythical formulations. The nuttier books on Mesoamerican culture are modern myths, thinly disguised as nonfiction accounts, created to satisfy the same essential human yearning for a paradisal condition and the promise of a life beyond the body—the same yearning that Mesoamerican civilization itself had pursued with such vigor through the centuries of its great metropolises. They, like us, suffered the same human frustrations and the same more-than-human dreams—and they, like us, more often than not got caught up in a confusion between worldly and spiritual meanings that prevented those frustrations from ever being authentically healed.

Like the popular conception of Pacal Votan's tomb lid as a space capsule, the frequent association of Mesoamerican civilization with the lost continent of Atlantis conceals an important psychological truth. Regardless of whatever historical validity there may be to stories of Atlantis and other such legendary places, the images these stories give us, of cities of incalculable harmony and perfection disappearing beneath the waves with the promise of their spires one day miraculously rising again into the light, repeat in slightly different terms the same essential myth that the Mesoamerican cities referred to constantly over the course of centuries. Those peoples longed, like ourselves, for a world of greater intensities than our own—a world only dimly remembered where everything had once appeared in the sharper focus that the godlike mortals of those times enjoyed. When the gods of the *Popol Vuh* created the first humans, they saw with such capacity. This, we are told, perturbed those gods, who were apparently nervous about what these new and inexperienced beings would do with such all-embracing force and wisdom. Therefore the visionary capacity of these newly created beings was reduced: their eyes were fogged up slightly by the gods, "as the face of a mirror is breathed upon. Their eyes were weakened. Now it was only when they looked nearby that things were clear."[13]

Now as then, when mortals look too far beyond the limits of the physical world their vision blurs, and the results of that blurring are frustrating to all who experience it. Atlantis, Wirikuta, Tlapallan: such places do not like to stay in focus. The vision needed to take in their fabulous details is not a simply human vision, and human beings can resort to every kind of foolishness in their attempts to change or deny this fact. Ancient Mesoamerica has for the past hundred years or so been a tremendously popular playground for such attempts. Now as ever, mortals wish to be as gods, and finding that they are not, look into the future and into the past for evidence that if they themselves are not, then perhaps someone else was or will be in their stead. Instead of these literalizing distortions of ancient mythic conceptions, instead of cheapening the harsh realities of the ancient world by turning it into a historical Eden, the modern with a desire to divinize the peoples of times past would do better to cultivate his or her own garden as it were—to examine with open eyes his or her own impoverished spirituality instead of indulging in feeble and groundless projections upon safely vanished ancient peoples.

The pyramids and temples of Mesoamerica were built not by gods but by a particularly inspired group of mortals, who spent over two thousand years demonstrating in a multitude of ways their frustrations with that condition. In the *Cantares* rituals, the last great proponents of this tradition of protest and desire for fuller dimensions of experience created, at tremendous risk to their own safety, a final demonstration of their unquenchable interest in this possibility by dressing up as angels and spinning from tethers attached to the tops of poles decorated as the cosmic tree that unites the worlds of gods and mortals.

In these ritual continuations of their former, war-oriented methods of attaining to the condition of godhood, the most devoted of these ritualists might now and then have achieved a moment of authentic visionary insight—a flashing glimpse of that world beyond the limits of the human condition which people of all times and places have sought and sometimes achieved. Though that vision stubbornly refused to remain with them for more than a moment, though it was replaced almost as soon as it arrived by the gray realities of their unenviable historical plight, it left these last, broken inheritors of the Mesoamerican spiritual tradition with an insight not to be argued with—an insight of a reality that is uncontestable if gone for the moment and destined, someday and somehow, to return.

The terms with which the Aztecs expressed this presentiment are of course no longer valid. The world conflagration that looms potentially in our own future is in no way a benevolent one, and any potentially happy revolution in cosmic realities will take place in interior regions and be framed in psychological terms. Nevertheless, this promise of greater things to come is a legacy that we troubled mortals of today would do well to value. It may be that in time we might find a way into and out of the transpersonal dimensions of human experience, expressed in our own terms and taking cognizance of our own very different realities, that would do justice to the ancient prophecies of a time at the end of time when the stars will fall from the sky and the lakes will once again become, as in Tranströmer's poem, windows into the earth.

Notes

Mesoamerican religion is extraordinarily rich in its terms of expression, and the most elementary introductions to it are twice the length of this book. I have resisted the temptation to cram these notes with passing references to all the aspects of this world not mentioned in the main narrative, for the result would have been a book composed more of notes than of actual text. What follows is a fairly casual selection of qualifications, quotes, references, and additional materials that didn't find their way into the main body of the text. Those who find notes tedious may safely ignore them.

Chapter 1: House of the Four Directions

1. Maya hieroglyphics were easily the most sophisticated pre-Columbian form of writing. Combining both phonetic and ideographic elements, they were at once an art form and an effective means of recording essential information. Likewise, the Maya's "dot and bar" numerical system—based on groups of twenty and incorporating a symbol for zero—was both a useful tool and a favored subject for intricate inscriptions. Dot and bar notations could be expressed simply for more practical reasons and complexly for more exalted ones—such as inscribing the date of the installation of a new ruler on a stone stela.

The Maya used their skills in writing and mathematics primarily to chart the movements of the celestial bodies, to record political events, and to parse and keep track of the unfolding of the days, months, years, and centuries of their calendar (one day = one kin; twenty days = one uinal, or "month"; 360 days = one tun, or year; 7,200 days = one katun, or "century," etc.). Obsessed with measurement, the Maya projected their calendar thousands of years into the past and the future, plotting the movements of celestial bodies like Venus with astonishing accuracy and meshing those movements into the tapestry of their ritual year. Like the later Aztec and other Mesoamerican peoples, the Maya used two calendrical systems at once. The first of these was the divinatory calendar, or almanac, made up of twenty "day names" and thirteen "day numbers." Each day saw the joining of a day name with a day number (the set of day names differing slightly depending on which civilization is in question). Day names were based on familiar objects, animals, or essential cosmic forces and prefixed by one of the thirteen day numbers to specify a single day in the calendar (e.g., One House, Nine Wind, Seven Death), which would not come again until 260 days had passed, at which point all the possible name and number combinations would have been used and the whole round would begin again.

The lore of this very ancient calendrical system is enormous and often quite complicated. Though the key numbers—20, 13, 260—seem arbitrary to us, they are believed to have been based on important characteristics of the terrestrial and celestial universes. The original Mesoamerican pantheon is thought to have contained thirteen gods, who perhaps each had a celestial reference in a certain constellation; men and women have twenty digits on their hands and feet; the incubation period for a human baby is about 260 days from the point of the first missed menses to birth.

The Maya and their neighbors also possessed the more conventional 365-day solar calendar used today, dividing it into eighteen months of twenty days instead of into twelve of thirty. The five days left over comprised a miniature month in themselves, and because of their extraneous nature were regarded as extremely negative days on which to do anything—especially to give birth. Children born on one of these days in Aztec times were known by a term translatable roughly as "useless person," and success for them in life was considered to be all but impossible.

2. Linda Schele and Mary Ellen Miller, *The Blood of Kings: Dynasty and Ritual in Maya Art* (New York: Braziller; Fort Worth, TX: Kimbell Art Museum, 1986), 15.

3. In his autobiography, the famous Sioux medicine man Black Elk gives an appealing description of his own people's conception of the directional life-transit of humans. Though it moves in a reverse direction than the Aztec version, the meaning is essentially the same: "Is not the south the source of life, and does not the flowering stick truly come from there? And does not man advance from there toward the setting sun of his life? Then does he not approach the colder north where the white hairs are? And does he not then arrive, if he lives, at the source of light and understanding, which is the east? Then does he not return to where he began, to his second childhood, there to give back his life to all life, and his flesh to the earth whence it came? The more you think about this, the more meaning you will see in it" (Black Elk, with John Neihardt, *Black Elk Speaks* [New York: Washington Square Press, 1972], 169).

4. Maya art is full of references to the watery nature of the underworld. Demons and underworld heroes are often portrayed with fins and gills, or as residing in giant seashells, which the inland Maya would have known about from trade with their coastal neighbors.

5. "House of Darkness and House of Light: Sacred Functions of West Mexican Funerary Art," in *Death and the Afterlife in Precolumbian America*, ed. Elizabeth Benson (Washington, DC: Dumbarton Oaks, 1972).

6. Ibid., 45.

7. Ibid.

8. Dennis Tedlock, trans., *Popol Vuh: The Definitive Edition of the Mayan Book of the Dawn of Life and the Glories of Gods and Kings* (New York: Simon & Schuster, 1985), 83.

9. My interpretation of this and the scene on the sarcophagus lid of the Temple of the Inscriptions is based on more detailed versions given in Schele and Miller's *The Blood of Kings.*

10. The warrior's human profile is visible, despite a mask he wears in the "X-ray" style frequently employed in Maya depictions of subjects in profile. The profile of this mask can be seen covering the warrior's face.

11. For an interesting scholarly treatment of the significance of the archetypal city in Mesoamerican history, as well as an analysis of the contradictions of the Aztec empire with a heavier concentration on historical detail than my own, see Davíd Carrasco, *Quetzalcoatl and the Irony of Empire* (Chicago: University of Chicago Press, 1982).

Chapter 2: The Star Beneath the Earth

1. For Eliade's ideas on this subject in his own words, see especially *Myths, Dreams, and Mysteries* (New York: Harper & Row, 1960). For the primitive, says Eliade, "any and every object may become an embodiment of the sacred. We have no right to infer from this any 'mental inferiority' on the part of the primitive, whose powers of abstraction and speculation have now been attested by so many observers. The 'nostalgia for Paradise' belongs, rather, to those profound emotions that arise in man when, longing to participate in the sacred with *the whole of his being*, he discovers that this wholeness is only apparent, and that in reality the very constitution of his being is a consequence of its dividedness" (p. 98).

2. I am here following some of the suggestions put forth in Karl W. Luckert's *Olmec Religion: A Key to Middle America and Beyond* (Norman: University of Oklahoma Press, 1976) about the snake's preeminent importance in Mesoamerican religious belief—an importance that Luckert believes eclipsed even that of the jaguar. Other writers disagree, citing the jaguar as the Olmecs' most religiously freighted animal. The problem is that Olmec and Maya sculpture is frequently so highly stylized that it is difficult to tell whether the animal-god represented is a snake or a jaguar or both. Luckert sees snakes everywhere in Mesoamerican art, and goes so far as to suggest that the Mesoamerican pyramid was itself a stylized snake head. This would seem dubious, and in the end the relative rank of these creatures in the eyes of the ancient Mesoamerican is not important: both were supremely significant because each demonstrated the combined qualities of beauty and danger so endemic to the natural world in general. Whether in the form of a giant cat or a snake, it is these qualities that are important in what follows.

3. Venus is the brightest body in the night sky besides the moon, and its 584-day cycle of disappearances and emergences was charted in detail by the Maya and other Mesoamerican peoples. This cycle is composed of four essential periods. For 236 days the planet is visible as the morning star, rising above the eastern horizon just ahead of the sun. For 90 days afterwards it remains invisible, appearing again above the western horizon as the evening star for another 250 days. Between the planet's disappearance as the evening star and its reemergence as the morning star, there passes another eight-day period of invisibility, during which the star was thought to "die" and be reborn somewhere beneath the surface of the earth. The importance of this mysterious planetary death and resurrection will become more apparent in the following pages.

4. Among many tribes animals were considered less as individuals than in terms of the species to which they belonged. The various species in this view were thought to have different methods of renewing themselves—the snake by shedding its skin, the game animal by regenerating from its bones, etc. Humans were sometimes said to have once possessed similar abilities, which long ago were lost through a slipup on the part of one of the first immortal humans.

5. "The Eskimo shaman Najagneq told the anthropologist Rasmussen that there was a supreme self which is "the inhabitant or soul (*inua*) of the universe. All we know is that it has a gentle voice like that of a woman, a voice 'so fine and gentle that even children cannot be afraid.' What it says is: *sila ersinarsinirdlige*, 'be not afraid of the universe.' " (Quoted in Ken Wilber, *Up from Eden: A Transpersonal View of Human Evolution* [Boston: Shambhala, 1986], 70.)

6. See, for example, the works of Stanislav Grof, John Weir Perry, and R. D. Laing.

7. Mircea Eliade, *Shamanism: Archaic Techniques of Ecstasy*, Bollingen series (Princeton: Princeton University Press, 1972), 293.

8. Ibid., 295.

9. The snake is itself one of the most intricately patterned of animals, and here again one sees how well it functioned as an all-embracing symbol of the universe, both the creator of order and the occasional destroyer of it.

10. This synopsis closely follows that provided by Dennis Tedlock in his translation of the *Popol Vuh*.

11. The fruit of the calabash is about the size of a human head; this is the first in a medley of human-vegetable references that occur throughout the story — references that date from the times when speculation about such similarities brought humans closer to the natural world instead of further away from it.

12. Tedlock, *Popol Vuh*, 133.

13. Rebirth from bones is an ancient concept: Paleolithic hunters are thought to have assembled the bones of their animal quarries in sacred spots in order that they would reclothe themselves with flesh and return renewed in the spring. This detail suggests that parts of the story of the twins' trip to the underworld date back to the very beginnings of human life in the Americas.

14. Tedlock, *Popol Vuh*, 153.

15. Ibid.

16. Ibid., 157.

17. Ibid., 158.

18. For a fuller consideration of human society as a clearing within a walled enclosure, and for one of the better of several recent creative interpretations of the significance of shamanistic thought for the modern world, see Hans Peter Duerr, *Dreamtime: Concerning the Boundary Between Wilderness and Civilization* (New York: Basil Blackwell, 1985).

19. Eliade, *Shamanism*, 36. The demons of the *Popol Vuh* are named after various human afflictions as well, but because humans no longer talk to them they use their mastery of these diseases purely to cause harm.

20. Ibid., 61.

21. Tedlock, *Popol Vuh*, 165.

22. Tomas Tranströmer, *Selected Poems: 1954–1986*, trans. Robin Fulton, ed. Robert Hass (New York: Ecco Press, 1987), 61.

23. As in the familiar Greek version of the tale, the protagonist is often unsuccessful in bringing the lost mate up out of the underworld once she is found. Like Orpheus, the hero commits a last-minute blunder that prevents his wife's complete reemergence into life. Nonetheless, the trip is in essence successful despite this loss, for it has functioned to initiate the hero into the mysteries of the afterlife and the possibility of a future resolution of the "problem" of death.

24. Tedlock, *Popol Vuh*, 114.

25. Quoted in Eliade, *Shamanism*, 326.

26. These platforms cannot be seen on the ruined pyramidal structures of today, for they were composed more often than not of wood and other perishable substances.

27. The degree to which the Aztecs—and particularly the Mexica—invested the sacrificial act with a personality of its own is demonstrated by their treatment of the stone knife, or *tecpatl*, with which heart sacrifice was performed. This knife was thought of as the "son" of the malevolent and powerful earth goddess Cihuacoatl. Like the rest of the Aztec gods, Cihuacoatl was always thirsty for human blood, and it was the job of her priests to secure it for her. When too many days had passed without sufficient bloodshed, these priests would drop an unsubtle hint to the rulers of the city by wrapping up the blood-encrusted knife as though it were a baby and leaving it untended in the crowded marketplace. "At the end of the day," writes Brundage (*The Jade Steps: A Ritual Life of the Aztecs* [Salt Lake City: University of Utah Press, 1985], 99), "the maternal feelings of the women would be aroused by the presence of a seemingly abandoned child among them, whereupon, opening the papoose, they would discover the repulsive *tecpatl* left there by the goddess as an earnest of her cruel hunger."

28. For a book-length, scholarly treatment of the Quetzalcoatl complex, see Burr Cartwright Brundage, *The Phoenix of the Western World: Quetzalcoatl and the Sky Religion* (Norman: University of Oklahoma Press, 1982).

29. Translated from the *Cantares Mexicanos* by Brundage in Brundage, *The Fifth Sun: Aztec Gods, Aztec World* (Austin: University of Texas Press, 1979), 208.

30. The equation of the dead warrior's spirit with a bird did not begin with the Aztecs but goes back at least to the Toltecs. However seriously the Toltecs themselves treated the idea, for the Aztecs it became an essential aid in validating the practice of warfare, and the most invested of Aztec warriors were most likely completely convinced of its truth. The warrior-spirit could take the form of a number of attractive Mexican species, but it was the hummingbird that was most often associated with the practice. "Why the hummingbird?" asks Jacques Soustelle (*The Four Suns: Recollections and Reflections of an Ethnologist in Mexico* [New York: Grossman, 1971], 173–74). "Because the hummingbird seems to go to sleep and die in the winter, only to be reborn in the spring, and so symbolized the

resurrection of the warrior who had been killed in battle or sacrificed." Certain species of hummingbird do in fact hibernate in the winter, an ability that the Dominican friar Fray Diego Durán remarked upon centuries ago, in his *Book of the Gods and Rites* (ed. and trans. Fernando Horcasitas and Doris Heyden [Norman: University of Oklahoma Press, 1971]). "For six months of the year," he writes of a certain Mexican species, "it is dead, and for six months it is alive. . . . When it feels that winter is coming, it goes to a perennial, leafy tree and with its natural instinct seeks out a crack. It stands upon a twig next to that crack, pushes its beak into it as far as possible, and stays there six months of the year—the entire duration of the winter—nourishing itself with the essence of the tree. It appears to be dead, but at the advent of spring, when the tree acquires new life and gives forth new leaves, the little bird, with the aid of the tree's life, is reborn. It goes from there to breed, and consequently the Indians say that it dies and is reborn. And with my own eyes I have seen this bird in winter with its beak thrust into the crack of a cypress, holding onto a branch as if it were dead, motionless. Having marked the spot, I returned in the spring when the trees had budded and become leafy, and I could not find it. I feel secure in writing this here, and I believe what the Indians told me. I praise the Almighty Omnipotent God, capable of performing even greater wonders!" (pp. 72–73).

31.   See especially Miguel Leon-Portilla, *Aztec Thought and Culture: A Study of the Ancient Nahuatl Mind* (Norman: University of Oklahoma Press, 1963).

32.   John (Fire) Lame Deer, with Richard Erdoes, *Lame Deer Seeker of Visions: The Life of a Sioux Medicine Man* (New York: Simon & Schuster, 1972), 200, 201, 208.

33.   The historical facts on which the story of the fall of Tula was based are extremely vague, but it is believed by some that the historical Quetzalcoatl Topiltzin might have been brought down from power by military/political forces outraged at his attempts to remove human sacrifice from the center of the city's program of action. The figure of Topiltzin might also have been represented in reality by a whole group of priests who had banded together to protest the barbarity of the sacrificial machine. Whatever the actual details of this drama were, they needn't interfere with the mythological rendition of the tale given here. Mythological and historical truth need not be antagonistic to one another, but ideally should be seen as two sides of one coin. The present account concentrates on the mythological side, and those readers interested in a more historical reading should consult the notes to John Bierhorst's "Quetzalcoatl," in his *Four Masterworks of American Indian Literature* (Tucson: University of Arizona Press, 1984) as well as David Carrasco's *Quetzalcoatl and the Irony of Empire.*

34.   John Bierhorst, ed. and trans., "Master Log," in *The Hungry Woman: Myths and Legends of the Aztecs* (New York: William Morrow, 1984), 52–55.

35.   "The Sorcerer's Dance," in ibid., 51–52.

36.   The implicit idea was that there was something missing in Topiltzin's revealed doctrine—a lack of spiritual authenticity that left it merely theoretical instead of authentically experiential. This cannot be proved, and it should be borne in mind that my reading of this story is speculative. Those interested in reading the story of Quetzalcoatl's Tula in its purest English rendering are referred to Bierhorst's translation, "Quetzalcoatl: An Aztec Hero Myth," in his *Four Masterworks*.

37. For details on this journey and its possible symbolism, see Bierhorst's "Quetzalcoatl" in his *Four Masterworks*.

38. Ocean and sky were often considered to be part of a single enfolding body of water in ancient Mesoamerica.

39. Translated as such in John Bierhorst, "Quetzalcoatl," in *Four Masterworks*, 51.

40. Bierhorst, *Four Masterworks*, 42.

41. Barbara G. Myerhoff, *Peyote Hunt: The Sacred Journey of the Huichol Indians* (Ithaca, NY: Cornell University Press, 1974), 124.

42. Ibid., 142–43.

43. Ibid., 143–45.

44. Ibid., 189.

45. Ibid., 183–84.

Chapter 3: The Hazardous World

1. The distinctly unbellicose Huichols are believed to have descended from the same general stock of desert wanderers as did the Aztecs; if this is the case, then generalizing about the specific character of the Chichimecs becomes all but impossible. This is perhaps all for the best, as attempts at tagging a group of people composed of distinct individuals as inherently warlike or peaceful (or worse, inherently "good" or "bad") inevitably oversimplifies complex human situations that can never be fully recovered. The most that can be said about those original northern populations is that something—be it a subtle degeneration in spiritual integrity or something as concrete as a prolonged absence of game animals—led to a disenchantment with their centuries-old lifestyle and a resultant openness to the possibilities of a mass descent into the more agriculturally viable lands to the south with widely divergent consequences.

2. The following several pages closely follow Burr Cartwright Brundage's narrative of the Mexica's early days in his *A Rain of Darts: The Mexica Aztecs* (Austin: University of Texas Press, 1972).

3. Huitzilopochtli was known to dress as a hummingbird, and his association, as the god of Aztec warfare, with this animal is interesting in connection to note 30 in chapter two about this animal's relationship to Toltec-Aztec conceptions of the warrior's paradisal afterlife.

4. Exceptions to the rule of course exist. History holds a number of examples in which a people become so swayed by eccentric religious or political motivations—which often include either explicitly or implicitly the promise of an eternal

afterlife—that they act with flagrant disregard for their own physical well-being. Even in this small group the Aztecs stand out, however, principally for the reason that their murderous tendencies were combined with a terrific intellectual and esthetic sensitivity uncommon in the majority of fanatical groups.

5. For an enlightening discussion of the different standard theories on motivations for the Aztec sacrificial craze, see Arthur Demarest, "Mesoamerican Human Sacrifice in Evolutionary Perspective," in *Ritual Human Sacrifice in Mesoamerica*, ed. Elizabeth Boone (Washington, DC: Dumbarton Oaks Research Library and Collection, 1984).

6. One of the many factors which together come to make urban lifestyles less spiritually viable is the fact that external security has the tendency to foster the illusion of internal security. If one's life is not in imminent danger every day, as it most likely was for the Chichimec wanderers who had to cope with the inconsistencies of weather and the constant movements of the food animals upon which they depended, the tendency arises to push away the question of mortality and with it the larger questions of human life and human death that the threat of mortality always engenders. The newly urbanized Aztecs' need for vivid displays of violence is partly explained by these peoples' semiarticulated recognition of this fact.

As an interesting aside, we might also mention here that in recent years, our own very comfortable culture has been forced to come to terms with its evasiveness of authentic spiritual questions through an encounter with the veterans of the Vietnam War. The current batch of books detailing the adventures of those veterans contain many eloquent examples of what can happen when members of a society cushioned against questions of human mortality—and hence the larger and more authentic world of spirit that can only be apprehended when the question of mortality is faced head-on—are suddenly confronted with a massive demonstration of the tenuousness of their own existence. Again and again in these accounts, the narrators describe the unreality of their first encounters with life-threatening situations, and the stranger sense of exaltation that further such encounters sometimes brought on. As these young men gradually came to terms with the overwhelming fact of human mortality, their interior acceptance of this fact sometimes led to an expanded dimension of experience, in which every detail in the world around them suddenly seemed to slide into sharper focus and their own sense of self seemed to expand beyond the limitations of time and place. Many times in these accounts there occur phrases like, "Suddenly I felt really alive for the first time in my life," or "For a second everything was more real." Unfortunately these sensations were short-lived, and upon returning to the reliable world of civilian life such individuals could become subject to fits of depression and exasperation, for the expanded sense of reality that battle had thrust upon them was now replaced by an experience of the day-to-day world as opaque, meaningless, and cut off from the larger world that accidentally and momentarily had been shown to them.

This odd intoxication, which these narrators describe themselves becoming attached to and which sometimes led them to deliberately seek out dangerous occupations when back in civilian life, can be taken as a simple, childish desire to experience feelings of omnipotence. Likewise, the sense of meaninglessness these veterans suffered once back in civilian life can be attributed to the complete rejection they so often received from a society that labeled them murderers and which made no effort to help them come to terms with the wounds, both physical and psychological, that they had suffered in the course of their time away. These are valid points of course—part of the complex web of psychological problems this war created for so many people—but the experience in question here is different from them, for it centers on a specifically felt sense of heightened reality that has nothing to do with fantasies of omnipotence and invulnerability but is actually much more sophisticated and potentially beneficial. Those who have reported it stress that they did not feel immune to death but totally conscious of it for the first time. Likewise, the depression suffered by these individuals upon their return centered not around the desperation or the loneliness of their situation but its unreality. It is interesting to keep these experiences in mind while examining the details of Aztec warfare, for the combination of exuberance and terror it engendered in the individual suggests that a parallel psychological process—at once liberating and intensely frustrating—was at work there as well.

7. Ernest Becker, *The Denial of Death* (New York: Free Press, 1973), 53–54.

8. For the Freudian, paradise is essentially intrauterine; the state of beatific one-ness with creation is concretized as the state of undisturbed slumber left behind when the infant passes through the gates of its mother's body. Though, at its strictest, psychoanalytical doctrine is less a help than a hindrance in understanding humankind's concealed desire for the angelic condition, that offshoot of psycho-analysis known as psychoanalytic anthropology (especially as practiced by Geza Roheim) has given many valuable insights into some of the themes being discussed here (see especially his *Gates of the Dream* [New York: International Universities Press, 1979]). For Roheim, and Freud's other more imaginative heirs, the shamanic dream-flight is a disguised return to the womb of the mother. It would be difficult to refute the evidence accumulated to corroborate this idea. (Why, to choose an example from Mesoamerica, does Quetzalcoatl penetrate the heavens as the "heart of the precious penis"?) The sexual-maternal imagery and scenarios uncovered by Roheim in fact only add to an appreciation of the depth of the shamanic drama; the only danger comes when we accept the Freudian interpretation as complete in itself.

Norman O. Brown's *Life Against Death: The Psychoanalytical Meaning of History* (Middletown, CT: Wesleyan University Press, 1959) and *Love's Body* (New York: Vintage Books, 1966) are obvious influences for the ideas in this book, with the important difference that Brown never cared much for speculations on the soul's independence from the body. His great post-Freudian formulations on hu-manity's recovery of the paradisal condition are strongly critical of what he calls "the traditional and stale notion that the psychic conflict in man is due to the ambivalence between his superorganic soul and his animal body" (*Life Against Death*, 82), and seek instead to "eliminate the mystery of the soul" through em-bracing mortality and living in a present freed from all fear for an abstracted future. Brown's critiques of Western doctrines of the soul may be correct, but it is unfor-tunate he never addressed the American Indian view of the soul, which at its best is capable of speaking of a life beyond the body without demeaning or running from the problematic integrity of physical, incarnate existence. Brown calls the shaman "the original sublimator, the historical ancestor of philosopher and prophet and poet," and suggests that "Platonism, and hence all Western philoso-phy, is civilized shamanism—a continuation of the shamanistic quest for a higher mode of being—by new methods adapted to the requirements of urban life" (*Life*

Against Death, 157–58). This sounds complimentary enough until we remember that for Brown sublimation is a negative term, implying an escape from the fact of mortality through mentally fabricated escape routes. Brown is ever in search of "bodily realities, not abstract intellectual principles," and for him the soul is always the latter: a fantasy designed by a consciousness afraid to die. From a sophisticated shamanic/American Indian perspective on the other hand, it can be something else entirely—the product not of an abstracting psyche afraid of death but the nucleus of the psyche itself, after it has faced and been transformed by an entrance into death through momentary departure from the physical frame.

9. "The Woman of Discord," in Bierhorst, *The Hungry Woman*, 75–80.

10. Durán, *Book of the Gods*, 174.

11. Ibid., 176.

12. Ibid., 179.

13. Ibid., 182.

14. Ibid., 184.

15. The notion that people capable of slicing off pieces of themselves are spiritual aristocrats—people whose superior concerns allow them to actively degrade concern for bodily safety—brings to mind the life of Vincent van Gogh. Other aspects of this painter's life—especially his infatuation with the sun—hold clues to unraveling the Aztec character that wait to be pursued. See George Bataille's interesting essay on this artist in his *Visions of Excess: Selected Writings, 1927–1939* (Minneapolis: University of Minnesota Press, 1985).

16. Brundage, *The Jade Steps*, 129.

17. Ibid., 48.

18. Ibid., 130.

19. Ibid., 47.

20. Ibid., 48–49.

21. The modern thrill-seeker, who works at a desk all week and pays large amounts of money to jump out of airplanes on the weekend, is to an extent a watered-down version of those figures, for the "release" he or she seeks from the constraints of the body is the same.

22. "The Fifth Sun," in Bierhorst, *The Hungry Woman*, 34–36.

23. Brundage, *A Rain of Darts*, 231.

24. One of Montezuma's last actions as king poetically underscores his reputed blindness to spiritual realities and his penchant for pursuing false, material symbols of immortality: following the example of several rulers before him, he ordered that his image be carved in stone on the face of the Rock of Chapultepec. Preserving the human face in stone is one of humanity's oldest and most favored methods of denying the inevitability of personal extinction, and that Montezuma should have ordered the construction of such an image when many more pressing matters were waiting to be dealt with shows the deeper motivations at work in him.

25. "The Talking Stone," in Bierhorst, *The Hungry Woman*, 87–92. The quotations from this story on the next several pages are also from this source.

26. "Montezuma's Wound," in ibid., 93–96.

Chapter 4: The Benevolent Apocalypse

1. In the days of Aztec supremacy, captured gods were often given much better treatment than the defeated mortals who had invented them. Idols taken from vanquished enemies of the Mexica were installed in an underground chamber at the heart of Tenochtitlan, where they were watched over by the earth goddess Cihuacoatl. Treated more like honored guests than as war booty, these idols were given offerings of blood and otherwise incorporated into Tenochtitlan's enormous schedule of ritual activities.

2. John Bierhorst, trans., *Cantares Mexicanos: Songs of the Aztecs* (Stanford, CA: Stanford University Press, 1985), 66.

3. Every fifty-two years (at the conclusion of the Aztec "century," when both the sacred almanac and the solar calendar had exhausted all their possible permutations and together began over again) the Aztecs' fixation with putting off the end of the universe was given its most elaborate formulation in the New Fire Ceremony. It was during this interval between "centuries" that the universe was in greatest danger of collapsing, and all the cities on the lake mobilized on the eve of the new year to fearfully wait to see whether the universe would be granted another fifty-two years of existence. The good-natured abandon that often accompanies primitive new-year-style celebrations was absent here, the focus being not on the potentially liberating qualities that the ending of time possessed but only on its negative, fearful ones.

4. Roman numerals cited in this chapter correspond to the numbers given the songs in Bierhorst's 1985 translation of the *Cantares Mexicanos*.

5. Diego de Landa, quoted by Alfred M. Tozzer in his "Landa's Relacion de las Cosas de Yucatan," in Elizabeth Boone (ed.), *Ritual Human Sacrifice*. The comment was originally made in reference to Maya heart sacrifice, not Aztec, but I take the liberty of using it here in an Aztec context.

6. Bierhorst, *Cantares Mexicanos*, 32.

7. Ibid.

8. A god of compassion such as the Spaniards claimed to offer in Jesucristo did not seem like such a bad idea to some Aztec individuals, and some *Cantares* songs seem to encourage complete acceptance of Christian doctrine not so much out of a desire to placate the Spaniards but because they were fed up with violence being the sole acknowledged means of entrance into the divine.

9. Suspicious and fearful as they were about the spiritual dimension in general, the Aztecs still managed to postulate an Eden-like primordial world as pleasant as that of the Huichols and other less negatively inclined native peoples. This region could be associated with Tlapallan or Tlalocan (the heaven of the drowned), but also was strongly associated with a place called Tamoanchan, whose name was

adopted by the Aztecs from Maya sources. According to Brundage, Tamoanchan originally meant "Place of the Moan Bird Serpent," and when the Aztecs described it they placed it in the sky just beneath Omeyocan, or "Place of Duality"—the pinnacle of the entire universe from which all creation had originally descended. According to legend, Xochiquetzal, one of several sex goddesses in the Aztec pantheon, had ripped a handful of blossoms from the flowery crown of the tree that bloomed perennially at the center of Tamoanchan and for this sexually flavored transgression she and all the other gods besides were cast down into the lower realms of struggle and hardship. The obvious biblical flavor of this story need not necessarily arouse suspicions of Spanish influence. The scope and integrity of the Fall myth on the American continent in the times before the Conquest has been massively catalogued, and minor questions of Christian influence can in no way account for all the permutations it has been given by diverse peoples from simple forest dwellers to urban giants like the Aztecs.

10.   In regard to the angelic/shamanic nature of the descending and ascending *Cantares* ghost-warrior, it might be illuminating to consider here two quotes from Eliade, whose ideas have helped give shape to so many of the speculations in these pages. "The motifs of flight and of ascension to Heaven are attested at every level of the archaic cultures," he writes, "as much in the rituals and mythologies of the shamans and the ecstatics as in the myths and folklore of other members of the society who make no pretense to be distinguished by the intensity of their religious experience. In short, the ascension and the 'flight' belong to an experience common to all primitive humanity. That this experience constitutes a profound dimension of spirituality is shown by the subsequent history of the symbolism of ascension. Let us remember the importance assumed by the symbols of the soul as a bird, of the 'wings of the soul,' etc., and the images which point to the spiritual life as an 'elevation,' the mystical experience as an ascension, etc. The amount of documentation now at the disposal of the historian of religions is such, that any enumeration of these motifs and these symbols would be likely to be incomplete" (Eliade, *Myths, Dreams, and Mysteries*, 105). The universal presence of the flight scenario, says Eliade a little later in this same work, "proves that the roots of freedom are to be sought in the depths of the psyche, and not in conditions brought about by certain historical moments; in other words . . . the desire for freedom ranks among the essential longings of man, irrespective of the stages his culture has reached and of its forms of social organization. The creation, repeated to infinity, of [the] countless imaginary universes in which space is transcended and weight is abolished, speaks volumes upon the true nature of the human being. The longing to break the ties that hold him . . . in bondage to the earth is not a result of cosmic pressures or economic insecurity—it is constitutive of man, in that he is a being who enjoys a mode of existence unique in the world. Such a desire to free himself from his limitations, which he feels to be a kind of degradation, and to regain spontaneity and freedom . . . must be ranked among the specific marks of man" (p. 106).

11.   There is no way of telling what such a singer actually experienced in the course of the ritual that went along with these songs, just as there is no way of telling what Lady Xoc "saw" in the smoke that rose from the burning bowl of bloodied paper strips in the scene captured by the Maya stonecutter on the Yaxchilán lintels, but there is no denying the importance that such visions held for each. Sacrifice and visualization of spirits went hand in hand for the Maya much

as they did for the Aztecs because together these potent psychological experiences created rifts and fissures in the increasingly hardening material world; openings through which the fires and lights of the world beyond could occasionally, if only momentarily, be glimpsed. For many it might be enough to say that the mysterious ritualists of the *Cantares* at best "imagined" the appearance of these vanished warrior spirits, perhaps with the help of peyote or hallucinogenic mushrooms. Yet to say that this world-shattering appearance was an induced delusion and leave it at that does not do justice to the legitimate, if alien, worlds of meaning that are in question here.

Western civilization has, since the beginnings of its contact with Indians, been alternately impressed and appalled by these peoples' frequently manifested ability to see and hear things that are simply "not there" for the Western observer. That ability cannot be swept under the rug as primitive naïveté, for the pursuit of visions is a central part of the practices of tribes across the span of the continent. Who do not accept those visions willy-nilly but subject them to rigorous scrutiny. Statements by Sioux and Huichol shamans on the subject stress the importance of differentiating between the simple psychological effects of drugs, exhaustion, and food deprivation, and the truly penetrating, truly consequential visions born of inspiration, talent, and stubborn determination.

Miracles and fantastic appearances are well attested to in the writings of all the world's major religious traditions, though as with interpretations of the *Cantares* they are often intentionally ignored by apologists who want these traditions' more philosophical concepts taken seriously and fear that they would be compromised or invalidated by elements of "primitive superstition." Some sects of mysticism tend to play down the independent reality of the visionary landscape out of fear that its wonders will detract the spiritual initiate from single-minded pursuit of release from the incarnate world, but among others, particularly the Sufis, this dimension is viewed with greater respect. Philosophers in that tradition, such as Avicenna and Ibn 'Arabi, created an extraordinarily sophisticated catalogue of visionary states, the subtlety and discernment of which is such that most contemporary writings on the transpersonal dimension read like primitive fumblings by comparison. Henry Corbin, the preeminent modern interpreter of this body of wisdom, coined the term "imaginal" to describe the general dimension of psychological experience that these philosophers address: the term's meaning and implications are extremely difficult to summarize, but essentially it refers to realms of psychological experience that are not simply subjective or objective but somewhere in between. In Sufi thought, it is not enough to say that a perceived reality is either real or imagined, for these cut-and-dried terms fail to address a limitless middle ground in which phenomena are both shaped by the imagination of the observer while at the same time existing independently of him or her.

Between the shores of the simply imaginary and the indisputably concrete lies an ocean of experience that, while partaking of a reality infinitely more profound and complete than the one revealed by ordinary daylight, does not like to manifest on command or hold still for measurement. This enhanced variety of imagining is extremely difficult to approach and describe, and Western psychology is only just beginning to come to terms with its implications. Corbin's work on this lost dimension of human experience marks the beginning of what might be one of the most challenging and fruitful psychological ventures of this century, and those skeptical of the revolutionary nature of his writings are urged to consult the works themselves. For our somewhat more superficial purposes it must be sufficient to point to them as a partial validation of some of the more extravagant claims made here about the integrity of Indian religious perceptions.

12. The hunger for such magical events is still very much alive. The popularity of Carlos Castaneda's first books on the Yaqui shaman Don Juan—who, it now appears, seems himself to have existed somewhere in the boundary between imagination and reality—had much to do with their convincing descriptions of "nonordinary reality," for they had the ability to open readers to the possibility of viable dimensions of experience existing behind the mundane. When Don Juan ripped the veil of Castaneda's perceptions of his world at the conclusion of *A Separate Reality*, the second book in the series, readers everywhere felt a secret surge of joy and recognition, and Castaneda's following books became enormous best-sellers. When the quality of Castaneda's books declined with later installments and Don Juan himself came more and more to be suspected of being a fabrication, many readers felt cheated and betrayed. But the quality of Castaneda's early books remains largely intact in spite of the disappointments of the later ones, for whether factual or not, the essential dramas they describe are real and important ones.

13. Tedlock, *Popol Vuh*, 167.

Bibliography

Bataille, Georges. *Erotism: Sensuality and Death*. San Francisco: City Lights Books, 1986.

_____. *Theory of Religion*. New York: Zone Books, 1989.

_____. *Visions of Excess: Selected Writings, 1927–1939*. Minneapolis: University of Minnesota Press, 1985.

Becker, Ernest. *The Denial of Death*. New York: Free Press, 1973.

Benson, Elizabeth P., ed. *Death and the Afterlife in Pre-Columbian America: A Conference at Dumbarton Oaks, October 27th 1973*. Washington, DC: Dumbarton Oaks Research Library and Collections, Trustees for Harvard University, 1975.

Bernal, Ignacio. *Mexico Before Cortez: Art, History and Legend*. New York: Anchor Books, 1973.

Berrin, Kathleen, ed. *Art of the Huichol Indians*. New York: Abrams; San Francisco: The Fine Arts Museums of San Francisco, 1978.

_____, ed. *Feathered Serpents and Flowering Trees: Reconstructing the Murals of Teotihuacan*. San Francisco: The Fine Arts Museums of San Francisco, 1988.

Bierhorst, John, trans. *Cantares Mexicanos: Songs of the Aztecs*. Stanford, CA: Stanford University Press, 1985.

_____, ed. and trans. *Four Masterworks of American Indian Literature*. Tucson: University of Arizona Press, 1984.

_____, ed. and trans. *The Hungry Woman: Myths and Legends of the Aztecs*. New York: William Morrow, 1984.

_____, ed. *In the Trail of the Wind: American Indian Poems and Ritual Orations*. New York: Farrar, Straus & Giroux, 1987.

_____, ed. *The Mythology of North America*. New York: William Morrow, 1985.

_____, ed. *The Red Swan: Myths and Tales of the American Indians*. New York: Farrar, Straus & Giroux, 1976.

_____, ed. *The Sacred Path: Spells, Prayers and Power Songs of the American Indians*. New York: Quill Books, 1983.

Black Elk (with John Neihardt). *Black Elk Speaks*. New York: Washington Square Press, 1972.

_____ (with Joseph Epes Brown). *The Sacred Pipe: Black Elk's Account of the Seven Rites of the Oglala Sioux*. New York: Penguin Books, 1971.

Bly, Robert. *The Kabir Book: Forty-four of the Ecstatic Poems of Kabir*. Boston: Seventies/Beacon Press, 1977.

_____. *Selected Poetry of Rainer Maria Rilke*. New York: Harper & Row, 1981.

_____. *Sleepers Joining Hands*. New York: Harper & Row, 1973.

Boone, Elizabeth, ed. *Ritual Human Sacrifice in Mesoamerica*. Washington, DC: Dumbarton Oaks Research Library and Collections, 1984.

Brotherston, Gordon. *Image of the New World: The American Continent Portrayed in Native Texts*. London: Thames and Hudson, 1979.

Brown, Norman O. *Life Against Death: The Psychoanalytical Meaning of History*. Middletown, CT: Wesleyan University Press, 1959.

_____. *Love's Body*. New York: Vintage Books, 1966.

Brundage, Burr Cartwright. *The Fifth Sun: Aztec Gods, Aztec World*. Austin: University of Texas Press, 1979.

_____. *The Jade Steps: A Ritual Life of the Aztecs*. Salt Lake City: University of Utah Press, 1985.

_____. *The Phoenix of the Western World: Quetzalcoatl and the Sky Religion*. Norman: University of Oklahoma Press, 1982.

_____. *A Rain of Darts: The Mexica Aztecs*. Austin: University of Texas Press, 1972.

Burkert, Walter. *Homo Necans: The Anthropology of Ancient Greek Sacrificial Ritual and Myth*. Berkeley and Los Angeles: University of California Press, 1983.

Campbell, Joseph. *The Hero with a Thousand Faces*. Bollingen series. Princeton, NJ: Princeton University Press, 1972.

_____, ed. *Myths, Dreams, and Religion*. Dallas, TX: Spring Publications, 1988.

_____. *Primitive Mythology*. Vol. 1 of *The Masks of God*. New York: Viking, 1970.

_____, ed. *Spiritual Disciplines*. Papers from the "Eranos Yearbooks." New York: Bollingen/Pantheon, 1960.

Carrasco, Davíd. *Quetzalcoatl and the Irony of Empire*. Chicago: University of Chicago Press, 1982.

Castaneda, Carlos. *Journey to Ixtlan: The Lessons of Don Juan*. New York: Simon & Schuster, 1972.

Coe, Michael. "Death and the Ancient Maya." In *Death and the Afterlife in Pre-Columbian America*, edited by Elizabeth P. Benson.

Coe, Michael. *Lords of the Underworld: Masterpieces of Classic Maya Ceramics*. Princeton, NJ: Princeton University Press, 1978.

Coe, Michael. *The Maya*. 4th ed. London: Thames and Hudson, 1987.

Coe, Michael, Dean Snow, and Elizabeth Benson. *Atlas of Ancient America*. New York: Facts on File, 1986.

Corbin, Henry. *Creative Imagination in the Sufism of Ibn 'Arabi*. Bollingen series. Princeton, NJ: Princeton University Press, 1969.

_____. *The Man of Light in Iranian Sufism*. Boulder, CO: Shambhala Press, 1978.

Davies, Nigel. *Human Sacrifice in History and Today.* New York: William Morrow, 1981.

_____. *Voyagers to the New World.* Albuquerque: University of New Mexico Press, 1979.

Deikman, Arthur J. *The Observing Self: Mysticism and Psychotherapy.* Boston: Beacon Press, 1982.

Demarest, Arthur. "Mesoamerican Human Sacrifice in Evolutionary Perspective." In *Ritual Human Sacrifice in Mesoamerica,* edited by Elizabeth Boone.

De Rougemont, Denis. *Love in the Western World.* New York: Pantheon, 1956.

Dodds, E. R. *The Greeks and the Irrational.* Berkeley: University of California Press, 1951.

Duerr, Hans Peter. *Dreamtime: Concerning the Boundary Between Wilderness and Civilization.* New York: Basil Blackwell, 1985.

Durán, Diego. *"Book of the Gods and Rites" and "The Ancient Calendar."* Translated and edited by Fernando Horcasitas and Doris Heyden. Norman: University of Oklahoma Press, 1971.

Duverger, Christian. "The Meaning of Sacrifice." In *Fragments for a History of the Human Body,* Part Three. Edited by Michael Feher.

Eliade, Mircea. *Birth and Rebirth: The Religious Meanings of Initiation in Human Culture.* New York: Harper & Row, 1958.

_____. *Cosmos and History: The Myth of the Eternal Return.* Bollingen series. New York: Harper & Row, 1959.

_____, ed. *From Primitives to Zen: A Thematic Sourcebook on the History of Religions.* New York: Harper & Row, 1967.

_____. *A History of Religious Ideas.* Vol 1 of *From the Eleusinian Mysteries to the Stone Age.* Chicago: University of Chicago Press, 1978.

_____. *Myth and Reality.* New York: Harper & Row, 1963.

_____. *Myths, Dreams, and Mysteries.* New York: Harper & Row, 1960.

_____. *Occultism, Witchcraft, and Cultural Fashions.* Chicago: University of Chicago Press, 1976.

_____. *Patterns in Comparative Religion.* Cleveland, OH: Meridian Books, 1963.

_____. *The Sacred and the Profane: The Nature of Religion.* New York: Harcourt, Brace & World, 1959.

_____. *Shamanism: Archaic Techniques of Ecstasy.* Bollingen series. Princeton, NJ: Princeton University Press, 1972.

_____. *The Two and the One.* Chicago: University of Chicago Press, 1979.

_____. *Yoga: Immortality and Freedom.* Bollingen series. Princeton, NJ: Princeton University Press, 1970.

Erdoes, Richard, and Alfonzo Ortiz. *American Indian Myths and Legends.* New York: Pantheon Fairy Tale and Folklore Library, 1984.

Feher, Michael, with Ramona Naddaff and Nadia Tazi, eds. *Fragments for a History of the Human Body.* Part Three. New York: Zone Books, 1989.

Furst, Peter T. "The Art of Being Huichol." In *Art of the Huichol Indians.* Edited by Kathleen Berrin.

_____, ed. *Flesh of the Gods: The Ritual Uses of Hallucinogens.* New York: Praeger, 1972.

_____. "House of Darkness and House of Light: Sacred Functions of West Mexican Funerary Art." In *Death and the Afterlife in Pre-Columbian America.* Edited by Elizabeth P. Benson.

_____. "Huichol Conceptions of the Soul." *Folklore Americas* 27 (June 1967): 39–103.

_____. *To Find Our Life: Peyote Among the Huichol Indians of Mexico.* In *Flesh of the Gods.* Edited by Peter T. Furst.

Girard, Rene. *Violence and the Sacred.* Baltimore: Johns Hopkins University Press, 1977.

Gossen, Gary H. *Symbol and Meaning Beyond the Closed Community: Essays in Mesoamerican Ideas.* Albany: Institute for Mesoamerican Studies, University at Albany, State University of New York, 1986.

Grof, Stanislav. *Beyond the Brain: Birth, Death, and Transcendence in Psychotherapy.* Albany: State University of New York Press, 1985.

Guss, David M., ed. *The Language of the Birds: Tales, Texts, and Poems of Interspecies Communication.* San Francisco: North Point Press, 1985.

Hans, James H. *The Play of the World.* Amherst: University of Massachusetts Press, 1981.

Hillman, James. *The Dream and the Underworld.* New York: Harper & Row, 1979.

Hillman, James. *Re-Visioning Psychology.* New York: Harper & Row, 1977.

Hillman, James. *The Thought of the Heart.* Eranos Lectures #2. Dallas: Spring Publications, 1984.

_____, and Heinrich Roscher. *Pan and the Nightmare.* Dallas: Spring Publications, 1979.

Hultkrantz, Åke. *Native Religions of North America.* San Francisco: Harper & Row, 1987.

_____. *The Religions of the American Indians.* Berkeley and Los Angeles: University of California Press, 1979.

Hyde, Lewis. *The Gift: Imagination and the Erotic Life of Property.* New York: Vintage Books, 1983.

Kalweit, Hulgar. *Dreamtime and Innerspace: The World of the Shaman.* Boston: Shambhala, 1988.

Krickeberg, Walter; Hermann Trimborn; Werner Muller; and Otto Zerries. *Pre-Columbian American Religions*. New York: Holt, Rinehart & Winston, 1969.

Krishna, Gopi, with James Hillman. *Kundalini: The Evolutionary Energy in Man*. Boulder, CO: Shambhala, 1971.

Lamb, F. Bruce. *Wizard of the Upper Amazon*. Berkeley, CA: North Atlantic Books, 1971.

Lame Deer, John (Fire), with Richard Erdoes. *Lame Deer Seeker of Visions: The Life of a Sioux Medicine Man*. New York: Simon & Schuster, 1972.

Larsen, Stephen. *The Shaman's Doorway: Opening Imagination to Power and Myth*. Barrytown, NY: Station Hill Press, 1988.

Laughlin, Robert M. *The People of the Bat: Mayan Tales and Dreams from Zinacantan*. Washington, DC: Smithsonian Institution Press, 1988.

Leon-Portilla, Miguel. *Aztec Thought and Culture: A Study of the Ancient Nahuatl Mind*. Norman: University of Oklahoma Press, 1963.

_____. *Pre-Columbian Literatures of Mexico*. Norman: University of Oklahoma Press, 1969.

Levi-Strauss, Claude. *Structural Anthropology*. New York: Basic Books, 1963.

Luckert, Karl W. *Olmec Religion: A Key to Middle America and Beyond*. Norman: University of Oklahoma Press, 1976.

Miller, Mary Ellen. *The Art of Mesoamerica from Olmec to Aztec*. London: Thames and Hudson, 1986.

Myerhoff, Barbara G. "Peyote and the Mystic Vision." In *Art of the Huichol Indians*. Edited by Kathleen Berrin.

_____. *Peyote Hunt: The Sacred Journey of the Huichol Indians*. Ithaca, NY: Cornell University Press, 1974.

Neumann, Erich. *The Great Mother: An Analysis of the Archetype*. Bollingen series. Princeton, NJ: Princeton University Press, 1972.

_____. *The Origins and History of Consciousness*. Bollingen series. Princeton, NJ: Princeton University Press, 1970.

O'Flaherty, Wendy Doniger. *Dreams, Illusion, and Other Realities*. Chicago: University of Chicago Press, 1984.

Ortiz, Alfonso. *The Tewa World: Space, Time, Being, and Becoming in a Pueblo Society*. Chicago: University of Chicago Press, 1969.

Perry, John Weir. *Roots of Renewal in Myth and Madness*. San Francisco: Jossey-Bass, 1976.

Plato. *The Collected Dialogues*. Edited by Edith Hamilton and Huntington Cairns. Bollingen series. Princeton, NJ: Princeton University Press, 1961.

Róheim, Géza. *The Gates of the Dream*. New York: International Universities Press, 1979.

Rothenberg, Jerome, ed. *Technicians of the Sacred: A Range of Poetries from Africa, America, Asia, Europe & Oceana.* 2d ed., rev. and exp. Berkeley and Los Angeles: University of California Press, 1985.

Roys, Ralph L. *Ritual of the Bacabs.* Norman: University of Oklahoma Press, 1965.

Sahagún, Bernardino de. *Florentine Codex: General History of the Things of New Spain.* Translated by Arthur J. O. Anderson and Charles E. Dibble. 10 vols. Santa Fe, NM: School of American Research; Salt Lake City: University of Utah, 1950–63.

Schele, Linda. "Human Sacrifice Among the Classic Maya." In *Ritual Human Sacrifice in Mesoamerica.* Edited by Elizabeth Boone.

Schele, Linda, and Mary Ellen Miller. *The Blood of Kings: Dynasty and Ritual in Maya Art.* New York: Braziller; Fort Worth: Kimbell Art Museum, 1986.

Scott, Mary. *Kundalini in the Physical World.* London: Routledge & Kegan Paul, 1983.

Sejourné, Laurette. *Burning Water: Thought and Religion in Ancient Mexico.* Translated from the Spanish by Irene Nicholson. New York: Vanguard Press, 1956.

Shah, Idries. *The Way of the Sufi.* New York: E. P. Dutton, 1970.

Snyder, Gary. *The Real Work: Interviews and Talks, 1964–1979.* New York: New Directions, 1980.

Soustelle, Jacques. *The Daily Life of the Aztecs.* New York: Macmillan, 1962.

————. *The Four Suns: Recollections and Reflections of an Ethnologist in Mexico.* New York: Grossman, 1971.

————. *The Olmecs: The Oldest Civilization in Mexico.* Norman: University of Oklahoma Press, 1985.

Sullivan, Lawrence. *Icanchu's Drum: An Orientation to Meaning in South American Religions.* New York: Macmillan, 1988.

Swann, Brian, and Arnold Krupat, eds. *Recovering the Word: Essays on Native American Literature.* Berkeley and Los Angeles: University of California Press, 1988.

Tedlock, Barbara. *Time and the Highland Maya.* Albuquerque: University of New Mexico Press, 1985.

Tedlock, Dennis. "Creation in the *Popol Vuh:* A Hermeneutical Approach." In *Symbol and Meaning Beyond the Closed Community: Essays in Mesoamerican Ideas.* Edited by Gary H. Gossen. Albany, NY: Institute for Mesoamerican Studies, 1986.

————. *Popol Vuh: The Definitive Edition of the Mayan Book of the Dawn of Life and the Glories of Gods and Kings.* New York: Simon & Schuster, 1985.

————. "Walking the World of the *Popol Vuh.*" In *Recovering the Word: Essays on Native American Literature.* Edited by Brian Swann and Arnold Krupat.

_____, and Barbara Tedlock, eds. *Teachings from the American Earth: Indian Religion and Philosophy*. New York: Liveright, 1975.

Thompson, J. Eric S. *Maya History and Religion*. Norman: University of Oklahoma Press, 1970.

Thompson, William Irwin. *Blue Jade from the Morning Star: An Essay and a Cycle of Poems on Quetzalcoatl*. West Stockbridge, MA: Lindisfarne Press, 1983.

Tompkins, Peter. *Mysteries of the Mexican Pyramids*. New York: Harper & Row, 1976.

Tozzer, Alfred M. "Landa's *Relacion de las Cosas de Yucatan*." In *Ritual Human Sacrifice in Mesoamerica*. Edited by Elizabeth Boone.

Tranströmer, Tomas. *Selected Poems: 1954–1986*. Translated by Robin Fulton and edited by Robert Hass. New York: Ecco Press, 1987.

Turner, Victor. *The Anthropology of Performance*. New York: P. A. J. Publications, 1988.

Wilber, Ken. *Up from Eden: A Transpersonal View of Human Evolution*. Boston: Shambhala, 1986.

Zimmer, Heinrich. *The King and the Corpse: Tales of the Soul's Conquest of Evil*. Princeton, NJ: Bollingen/Princeton University Press, 1971.

_____. *Philosophies of India*. Bollingen series. Princeton, NJ: Princeton University Press, 1969.

Index